The History *of the* World According *to* Me

Jill Kavalek

The History of the World According to Me
Copyright © 2021 by Jill Kavalek

All rights reserved. No part of this publication may be reproduced, distributed, or transmitted in any form or by any means, including photocopying, recording, or other electronic or mechanical methods, without the prior written permission of the author, except in the case of brief quotations embodied in critical reviews and certain other non-commercial uses permitted by copyright law.

Tellwell Talent
www.tellwell.ca

ISBN
978-0-2288-6669-5 (Paperback)
978-0-2288-6670-1 (eBook)

I dedicate this book to Ray Kolle, who has always been there for me. I am grateful to him for editing the book, and to his son, David Kolle, for the charming drawings.

Jill Kavalek

TABLE OF CONTENTS

Introduction vii

Chapter 1   The Bible and Very Early Bits and Pieces 1
Chapter 2   The Egyptians and more of the Bible 8
Chapter 3   Jesus 12
Chapter 4   More about How the Three Major Religions got
            Started 16
Chapter 5   Charlemagne 20
Chapter 6   England and its Various Goings-on until Magna Carta ...21
Chapter 7   More about The Knights Templar 27
Chapter 8   The Habsburgs 29
Chapter 9   Just a Few Pieces of Information 33
Chapter 10 The Hundred Years War 36
Chapter 11 The War of the Roses 39
Chapter 12 Ferdinand and Isabella 41
Chapter 13 The Catholics, Martin Luther and Henry VIII 43
Chapter 14 The Muslims, Martin Luther and Bloody Mary 47
Chapter 15 Elizabeth 49
Chapter 16 Mary Queen of Scots 52
Chapter 17 James I of England and VI of Scotland 56
Chapter 18 Charles I, the Civil War, Oliver Cromwell and Tulips 58
Chapter 19 Louis XIV 61
Chapter 20 The Devil's Number 64
Chapter 21 James II 68
Chapter 22 William and Mary 70
Chapter 23 Queen Anne and the Spanish War of Succession 72
Chapter 24 Peter the Great 76

Chapter 25   More Historical Trivia that Struck Me as Interesting....80
Chapter 26   The Georges..82
Chapter 27   The War of Jenkins' Ear and Other Peculiarities..........86
Chapter 28   Rebellions and Other Goings-On..................................91
Chapter 29   More Trivia 93
Chapter 30   Louis XV..94
Chapter 31   Catherine the Great..98
Chapter 32   The Industrial Revolution 100
Chapter 33   The Americans..102
Chapter 34   Australia...106
Chapter 35   The Habsburgs Again...109
Chapter 36   George III and the Prince Regent................................113
Chapter 37   The French Revolution...116
Chapter 38   Napoleon 119
Chapter 39   Josephine 127
Chapter 40   Lady Hamilton and Nelson..130
Chapter 41   Princess Charlotte 135
Chapter 42   King William IV..137
Chapter 43   A Few Things I Find Odd and/or Entertaining 140
Chapter 44   The Rothschilds..144
Chapter 45   The Sassoons...147
Chapter 46   The British East India Company 149
Chapter 47   Odds and Ends...151
Chapter 48   The Victorians..153
Chapter 49   American Civil War...163
Chapter 50   The Suffragettes...165
Chapter 51   The Gold Rush 167
Chapter 52   Emperor Franz Joseph of Austria...............................169
Chapter 53   Edward VII..175
Chapter 54   The lead up to, and aftermath, of World War I 176
Chapter 55   Russia 181
Chapter 56   More about the Jews..183
Chapter 57   The 1920's, 1930s, and 1940s....................................185
Chapter 58   The Second Front..193

INTRODUCTION

Who am I to tell people about history? Well, I'm Jill Kavalek, a screenwriter and playwright.

(above: Jill Kavalek)

I've always liked history, though not so much acts of parliament and laws of the land and such. Well, the Corn Laws were quite interesting in a boring sort of way; a bit like sitting through something by Wagner. You find yourself thinking, "Is this never going to end?"; especially if you happen to get yourself tangled up in "The Ring Cycle"!

As a writer I probably have a quirky sort of mind and I like odd things… things that happened about history, in history, while the people that instigated them were thinking about something completely different.

I remember doing a history exam, and while cramming for it I was also reading a book about gnomes. Naturally, by the time the exam came along, I knew all there was to be known about gnomes and just managed to scrape through my history exam.

Most people (unless they are actually interested) know bits and pieces about history, but they often get them muddled up. For instance, I was at the dentist yesterday and he was convinced Peter the Great was French!

My step-grandson has just asked me why I have ignored the Hittites. Frankly, I'd never heard of the Hittites! And now that I've looked them up, I know why - despite being around for ages, none of them seem to have done anything interesting (apart from fight with the Egyptians, but everyone did that). I'm sorry, but there didn't appear to be one that stood out in the whole lot (though I have lately learnt that Abraham bought his grave from a Hittite, so, as far as I can see, the Hittites may have been all over the place as a sort of ancient Real Estate Agent office).

So, this is my (informal) History of the World, excluding - sad to say - The Hittites.

No wonder people get confused about history. I mean, Hollywood has a lot to answer for when it comes to historical drama; they tend to add things just to make the film or whatever more dramatic (as though the entire thing wasn't dramatic enough without the screenwriter adding his feelings on the subject and then the director taking it even further).

There's a popular belief in the film world that producers had a very hard time making Cecil B. De Mille (a very famous film director in his day) from keeping Moses out of "The War of the Roses." They probably need not have bothered, the general public wouldn't care as all his films were big and glossy (and seem to have featured Charlton Heston).

The other day I had the radio on and I was vaguely listening and I hear them talking about the Old Testament and someone said Isaac became Jacob. I blinked - what? Then trolling through the internet I discovered someone had asked who was Abraham's father; the reply was, "Ishmael". "Oh, no, no, no!" I said to my computer, "Well, not unless they're talking about the character in Moby Dick. I have no idea who he was the father of." But I'm pretty sure they meant the Biblical Ishmael and that's when I thought, "Someone really does have to make it their business to sort this lot out. It's about time we put Moses back in the Bible and the War of the Roses in the middle ages where they belong. And, as no one is beating down my door wanting me to write anything, it might as well be me who has a go at it." Not that I'm a professor of history or anything so important; as I said I am a writer (hopefully an amusing one), with credits mainly for writing plays and stuff for T.V., so you can expect a lot of "He said/they said".

I hope my rather individual and somewhat erratic version of history - or what I remember of it - will interest and entertain people while getting everyone more or less in their proper place in the scheme of things as they were doing whatever it was they did to make themselves memorable. A lot of history is amusing but you actually have to know something about history to be able to see what's funny about it.

For instance, Queen Anne is nearly always referred to as "the dead queen". Of course, she's dead - she's been dead for hundreds of years - but she was alive at one stage, so it's funny she's become most well-known for being dead. Later, I'll explain why.

As for this little epic of mine, fear not! All you are required to do is read; there will be no follow-up exam. As I am a simple so ul, you won't be deeply immersed in acts of parliament and other events (which I usually find dull). What I most remember about history are things I've either found strange, funny, brilliant or just plain daft.

By the way, do not look for chronological order all the time. As something pops into my head, I will write it in and later on, where it actually fits in, I'll explain it in greater detail, so it should make sense (at least mostly). As I said, I am not an historian (as neither was the Duke of Norfolk, but he does crop up a lot as we go along).

Jill Kavalek

CHAPTER 1

The Bible and Very Early Bits and Pieces

Firstly, let me say that prior to King David there is no archaeological proof that any of the characters in the Bible actually existed. However, as many of them were extremely interesting, doing fascinating things, let's go with the Bible. You can believe or not, as you see fit.

So to begin, we have to go back several thousand years to Abraham, who seems to be the first person who believed in one God. Until then most people were in tribes of various sorts and had a variety of gods (for different purposes). For example, there was Hestia, the Goddess of the hearth, whose name later became a well-known bra company! Some of the gods were nice and cute, such as Eros (now commonly known as Cupid), who went around darting people with love arrows. There was also Diana the Huntress, another one who had a way with arrows. Most of them seemed to have been pleasant enough, but then there were a few that were definitely not, like the God of War, Mars - or is it Ares? I can never remember which were Greek and which were Roman, and there's no point in getting into it now as I'm bound to get it wrong.

In the Middle East there were many small tribes. They also had gods but they seem mainly to do with the house and had unpronounceable names. Of course, there were also empires such as the Byzantines, who stuck around for a long time and only sort of collapsed once the Christian religion took hold under Emperor Constantine.

And then there were whole nations such as the Babylonians, the Philistines (and presumably the Hittites were in there somewhere), and, naturally, the Egyptians, who never disappear from history, no matter what seems to have been done to them, which reminds me of the Duke of Norfolk, but he comes in much later.

Supposedly, it was about then that along came Abraham. As I said, he was apparently the first person to believe in just the one God. The reason this came about was that the head of another tribe decided to burn him to death. In the middle of the fire God suddenly spoke to Abraham: "I am the one and only true God and he who believes in me will prosper. Walk out of the flames." Well, prospering seemed like a good idea, and walking out of the flames seemed an even better one. So, out he walked, not a mark on him, much to the annoyance of the tribal leader who had rather thought of himself as the chief and was proving it by doing away with Abraham. Abraham was adamant he had heard the word of the one true God and he was there to prove it, unscathed.

Abraham and his wife Sarah desperately wanted a child, although - according to the Old Testament - Abraham was a hundred years old by this time. He already had a son, Ishmael, with an Egyptian servant girl, Hagar.

After much praying, gnashing of teeth and weeping, etc., God eventually granted Sarah's wish and she had a son, whom they named Isaac. However, God wanted to be sure Abraham really did believe in Him, so He said, "You will sacrifice your son to me."

Sarah was beside herself. "He wants you to what?" she screamed at Abraham as he prepared for the sacrifice. "What's wrong with a goat?"

After all the performance to get her beloved son, now this? Finally, she muttered, "Well, you'd better be right!"

As I discovered while talking to a student of the Talmud, Isaac was actually thirty-seven when all this was going on (and had a son of his own, Jacob) and when he finally spoke up, you can imagine the conversation: "Excuse me... What? For thirty-seven years we've all done everything He wants, now He says sacrifice me? I don't think so!" But Abraham was determined to obey God's word and began sharpening his knife.

Then God finally spoke up, saying, "Stop! I just wanted to make sure you would obey My will. A goat will do, though I'd prefer a ram if you have one."

Sarah glared at Abraham, "What about a bunch of flowers? A ram's so expensive."

God spoke again, "By the way, I'd like Isaacs' son Jacob to change his name to Israel." Isaac considered the matter and thought that compared with offering his son up as a sacrificial lamb changing his name was definitely far more agreeable.

"Is he asking other people to do peculiar things too?" asked Sarah.

"He is the one God and must be revered in all things," Abraham replied.

"That's all very well, as long as He doesn't keep wanting us to sacrifice any of our children, or keep changing their names!" retorted Sarah.

However, Jacob on went on being Jacob until he apparently had a fight with an angel. What he wanted to fight with an angel for, I have no idea, but then I have no idea why half the world does what it's doing. Whatever his name was, Jacob came to no harm. Of course, we don't know what happened to the angel.

Again God spoke, "Jacob - now Israel - is going to be the father of the twelve tribes of Israel". (What He failed to mention was how many wives this concerned, or the fact he had to fight with an angel first.)

Now that Sarah had her own son, Hagar and Ishmael were surplus to requirements and she banished them, but God told Ishmael not to worry as his descendants would one day become a great nation.

As it turned out, Jacob - now Israel - had two wives and more children than the twelve required by God, including a girl. Two of the tribes broke away, making up the tribes of Israel and Judea, the main source of the Jewish religion. To be a Jew one has to have a Jewish mother. Because Hagar was Egyptian, her son Ishmael was also an Egyptian, so it was from him that we eventually saw the birth of the Muslim religion. But before that, along came Jesus of Nazareth and we got Christianity. (From these beginnings, came the three major world religions: Judaism, Christianity, and Islam.)

As Jacob - now Israel - aged he had plenty of children. One, named Judea, thought it might be nice to have a tribe of his own. It was really a bit like the Scottish clans, without skirts and the "Mac". Still under the umbrella of Abraham's one God making up the tribes of Israel and Judah, we have the main source of the Jewish religion. From Jacob - now Israel - we get the twelve tribes of Israel, one of them being led by Joseph (of the coat of many colours and Andrew Lloyd Webber fame). I'm not going into all their names because I can't remember them, but I know another son was called "Levi". The Levi's were not allowed to own land, but they could have cities. Which makes no sense at all to me, but that's what it says in the Old Testament.

Because Joseph was the youngest and was Israel's favourite son, the rest ganged up on him and sold him into slavery to the Egyptians, naturally, as any loving brothers would. However, when he arrived in Egypt, he began having dreams and visions, and predicted there would be famine and seven plagues. He became a big success with the Egyptians; because of Joseph and his dreams they were able to stock up on food and whatever else the dreams told them they would need.

The Egyptians thus survived with ease what was a terrible time for everyone else. Joseph's brothers came begging for help, which he eventually gave them, but somehow or other all of them ended up in slavery for many years. So, you see, things do have a habit of coming back to bite you.

Ten of the twelve tribes managed to disappear at some stage, only to be brought together later on by King David into two tribes, the Israelites and the Judeans.

And then, along came Moses.

Whether he was actually found among the bulrushes on the Nile by Pharaoh's daughter is a moot point (but it makes a cute illustration).

Anyway, when he was somewhat older he led the Jews out of Egypt. Before they left, the Lord told them to paint the blood of a lamb on their doors. When the Angel of Death came, he would pass over every Jewish house with the cross of blood on its door while every house without a cross would lose its first born. Hence, we got Passover.

It is entirely possible that the Red Sea did part because around that time a tsunami was reported somewhere off India, making waves all over the place - and maybe even leaving a convenient patch of dry Red Sea bed for Moses, et al. Moses and the Jews wandered around in circles in the Sinai desert for forty years. (The idea was apparently that the older generation who were used to being slaves would die out.)

Moses went up Mount Sinai and, after a chat with a burning bush, came back with the Ten Commandments that form the basis of the Torah and the Jewish religion.

While Moses was talking to the burning bush his tribes-people got bored and decided to build a Golden Calf. (Now I feel that has to be apocryphal; they were slaves for God's sake, so where did they get enough gold to build anything?)

Anyway, when Moses came down from the mountain with the Ten Commandments he found all his tribe dancing around a golden calf. God was furious and stormed at them: "What part of 'I am the Lord Thy God and you shalt not worship false idols', did you not understand?"

Everyone was very sorry but it had been a bit boring with Moses away and they thought God might like a nice golden calf.

"Well, I don't!," God replied.

The punishment was that Moses - after all that walking around - should never see the Promised Land. (To me, that actually seems a bit harsh, as he was away busily talking to the burning bush while all this calf-making was going on.)

Joshua took charge and they set off for the promised land of Canaan. When they reached Jericho, Joshua blew his trumpet and the walls came tumbling down (another good song).

CHAPTER 2

The Egyptians and more of the Bible

The Egyptians were enormously interesting. They were around from very early on, but despite all the various wars and people trying to take them over, they still managed to always be called "Egypt" and have Pharaohs, built pyramids, and nobody was able to subdue them for any length of time (though they did fall into decline when the Ottomans took them over). It was only thousands of years later when Napoleon arrived and discovered the Rosetta Stone - which gave them the key to reading ancient Egyptian hieroglyphics - that it was realised how important the Egyptians had actually been in the scheme of things.

Long before that the Jews decided that what they needed was a king; before that they had prophets. So, God said, "Okay, okay they want to be kings, personally I prefer prophets, but kings, hum, let them be kings."

The first king was Saul, who didn't seem to do very much. He had a son Jonathan who was friendly with a shepherd boy, David. David was very musical; not only that he was a black-belt major with a sling-shot which turned out to be a very good thing.

At the time the Philistines were having one of their fights with the Jewish tribes, and had what they regarded as their major weapon, a huge giant called Goliath. As David and Goliath faced each other, Goliath laughed down at the young boy from his huge height. David took aim with his sling-shot and whirled it above his head. Whoosh! One dead giant. The Jews won.

After more fighting (with all sorts of people, in which Saul and his son Jonathan were killed), David became king. He got the twelve tribes together and regained Jerusalem and for the first time Jerusalem became a sovereign state in its own right. That is why to this day it's called "Royal David's City".

Then there was Solomon. He was supposedly very wise about what you do if you have two women claiming a baby is theirs: you obviously cut it in half and the woman who says, "No, let the other woman take the baby," is the rightful mother.

He also built the first temple, which was promptly knocked down by Nebuchadnezzar of Babylonia. Then Solomon blotted his copybook by an affair with the Queen of Sheba and having a child by her. (One of my friends reading this said he was sure no one at that time would've been upset with this; they were all small tribes, Solomon was the king and they were always having affairs, and where was this place called "Sheba", anyway?)

Then, Cyrus the Great popped up. No one (unless you are a Biblical student) appears to have heard of him; a bit like me and the Hittites, I suppose, but Cyrus seems to have done a lot more than they did. Apparently, he took over most of the known world. He had Jewish blood and wherever he went he freed the Jew from slavery.

This was probably the beginning of Jews living in all sorts of countries, trying to keep their heads down, while living a quiet life, and only attacking if they were attacked. Cyrus respected the various countries' customs, and appears to have been quite a nice man. When he arrived in Jerusalem and discovered Nebuchadnezzar had knocked down Solomon's temple, he immediately had it rebuilt and tidied up the place. Obviously, he liked things nice and tidy - a sort of conquering interior (and exterior) decorator. He'd take over countries, tidy them up to his satisfaction and then move on to the next one (basically letting them rule themselves).

Time passed, and along came Alexander the Great. He was from Macedonia, which later became Greece and everybody knows about him. He began trying to take over the whole world, enslaving the Jews yet again although he didn't actually harm them too much. He also took over Egypt. His empire couldn't have lasted too long as the poor man died when only thirty-two.

The Greeks also had a whole bunch of gods who lived on Mount Olympus. As you may recall, I always get them muddled up in terms of which ones are the Greek and which ones are the Roman gods. Incidentally, I'm not sure where the Roman gods lived but I don't think it was on a mountain. However, I know one of them lived in the sea. He was, of course, Neptune. That's one I do know is Roman, the Greek version was Poseidon. And they both carried a large toasting fork; it seems to be a prerequisite for Gods of the sea, though what they find to toast down there I can't imagine. One's now a planet, the other a ship that sunk upside down. A friend of mine was in the movie.

Greece was the cradle of civilisation, producing people such as Homer, Socrates, Aristotle and Pythagoras (whom I could have well done without at school), and several other probably equally important personages that I have forgotten.

All I know about Hannibal was that he walked a whole bunch of elephants over the Pyrenees and the Alps and had something to do with the second Punic War. As I didn't even know they had a first one, I think it's best to leave well enough alone. It must have been an extreme effort with all those elephants; I imagine they were a sort of tank of their day.

Back in Jerusalem, the Romans had taken over. Things went reasonably calmly until Caligula wanted to put a statue of himself in the Temple. Knowing how cross God usually got about these things, the Jews stood out against it and consequently the second temple got pulled down.

What generally happened when Rome colonised a place was that they would put someone in charge with a token legion of soldiers while the place basically went on its merry way leaving the people that they had conquered much better off (with indoor plumbing and all sorts of things) without too much interference. So long as the citizens paid taxes to Rome, things went on relatively smoothly, but the Jews in Jerusalem wouldn't do this. They kept revolting until the Romans got so infuriated that they practically razed Jerusalem to the ground.

It dumbfounded them that the Jews who were living there should want their city back and, rather than accept defeat, took themselves off to Masada and - after a long siege - killed themselves to avoid being taken captive. Such a thing baffled the Romans.

What I don't understand is why on earth when the Roman Empire finally did crumble, they kept the straight roads but did away with indoor plumbing! By the same token, when did "Romans" suddenly become 'Italians'? I mean, the easy-going sort we know today. For hundreds of years they were conquerors of a great deal of the world, then all of a sudden they were "Italians". Organised, they are not. They haven't had a proper government for years. You get a group of Italians together and generally chaos ensues. I love Italy and the Italians, but they seem to live their lives with a sort of shrug-of-the-shoulder and an attitude of "what happens, happens", as though it's nothing to do with them. My ex-husband was staying at a hotel in Rome and there was a parking spot outside, so he asked if it was alright to park there. "How long you stay?" asked the well-meaning, affable local. "You say, it's a four days, si? Hmmm…should be fine. Four weeks, you could have a problem."

And that's Italians for you. However, this hasn't stopped them producing Renaissance men like Michelangelo, Galileo, and da Vinci, plus brilliant musicians, glorious cities, and some great fashion. It seems one doesn't have to be organised to make the world a more beautiful place.

CHAPTER 3

Jesus

(As I am Jewish, I will admit to not being an authority on Jesus, and only write from my point of view. I don't intend to offend anyone of any religion anywhere, so please forgive me if I do.)

God sent the Angel Gabriel down to Mary and told her she was going to have a baby but not to be frightened.

"But, how? I haven't..."

"It's all right He will be the son of God and Joseph is going to marry you. Everything is arranged."

Actually, everything wasn't arranged because at the time the Romans were having a head count and everyone had to go back to register in their original village. This meant total havoc all around, and then there was nowhere for Mary and Joseph to stay when they arrived in Bethlehem, their original village. (All of which only enforces my belief that it's always good to book ahead.) So Jesus was born in a somewhat crowded stable, surrounded by three kings, several shepherds, and an assortment of farm animals. From these events we eventually got Christmas.

Jesus was actually born sometime in April, but as he also died in April the powers-that-be thought that as the Pagans had a nice festival going in December to welcome in the winter, why not make his birthday then and combine the two?

(The Yule tree - actually, a Yule log, big enough to burn for the twelve days of Christmas - was already part of the pagan festival, but what we call a "Christmas tree" came care of Prince Albert, of Victoria and Albert fame. There was a Saint Nicholas floating about who gave presents to children, but the chubby-faced, bewhiskered Father Christmas as we know him now came from a Coca Cola ad sometime in the twenties. (I have no idea where we got bon-bon crackers.)

I believe that Jesus was born a Jew and died a Jew; I think he was a prophet and probably a healer. His first adult appearance on the scene to any degree was when he threw the money changers out of the temple. I imagine his plan was to try and tidy up his own religion and get rid of things that he felt were patently obsolete.

He spent forty nights in the desert, neither eating nor drinking, wrestling with his conscience as to what he should do. He was well aware that suggesting changes to any part to his religion would infuriate those above him in the synagogue. Though he felt God had sent him to do his bidding, I really don't think he had any intention of producing a completely new religion. In fact, he said as much.

Forty seems to be a thing with the Jews. There was Moses walking them around the Sinai for forty years, and now Jesus walking in the desert for forty days - an excursion that gave us Lent, although what pancake Tuesday has to do with anything, I'm not sure.

The Jews were happy to be left alone, but they were warriors, they had to be, fighting off all the various people who enslaved them. They weren't crazy about the Romans, nor the Philistines, nor the Babylonians, and several other people, all of whom seemed at one time or other to have turned them into slaves. They were waiting (and still are) for a Messiah who in their mind would bang a lot of heads together and would prove in some way to the Jews that they deserved a country of their own. This would not necessarily make them a power to be reckoned with; they just wanted to live their life their own way without interference from others.

Jesus didn't seem to fill the bill; he was a prophet, but then they were used to them. And with Jesus it was all this sweetness and light, which to the Jewish mind wasn't really getting them anywhere. Feeding hordes of people on two fishes and a couple of loafs of bread, raising people from the dead, and all this healing business… (it was at least two thousand years before "My son, the doctor" was the thing to be). It was stirring up the people and causing too much of a fuss.

When asked for taxes, the Jews refused to pay because all the coinage had on it the head of the Emperor and there was God's dislike of graven images. (God had got very cross with the Jews about graven images and various other things at one stage and did all kinds of drastic things to pull them back into line, so they were wary.)

Jesus, however, replied, "Give unto Caesar what belongs to Caesar." That didn't please the Jewish people either. They wanted someone who would stand up for the Jews, and possibly hit people when necessary. What they got was not only "Love thy neighbour" but also "Love thy enemies", which didn't go down so well. Why be nice to people who are not nice to you?

Jesus gathered around him twelve disciples, and his following began to grow. Herod's nose got right out of joint when some people started to refer to Jesus as King of the Jews. As far as Herod was concerned, he was king of the Jews, no one else.

Furthermore, the Romans became irritated with the whole lot of them when they began referring to Jesus as the Messiah. They captured Jesus, but not knowing what to do with him they tried giving him back to the Jews, but this was not the sort of Messiah most of them wanted, and now he was supposed to be King of the Jews; Herod was bad enough.

The Romans looked at each other, "What were they supposed to do?". They couldn't really see anything wrong with the man. He didn't want to fight with them, but he was causing a commotion with his growing band of followers; they had to do something.

The Last Supper was Jesus and his disciples celebrating Passover, and then he was betrayed by Judas for thirty pieces of silver. The Romans took him, and - as they didn't know what else to do with him - crucified him. And it's called "Good Friday"!

(Later, Peter, one of Jesus's closest disciples, decided when it was his turn to be crucified that he'd have it done upside down. Don't ask me why.)

The Romans assumed the rabble would disappear once Jesus was out of the way, but the they had forgotten the cardinal rule that a martyr soon becomes a symbol that creates a new following. With a crucified Jesus they had on their hands a bona fide reason for someone to start a new religion.

Then Jesus apparently rose from the dead (so why isn't it called "Good Sunday"?) and it was a whole new ball game!

This in time gives us Easter. There was already a pagan festival for the rites of spring and fertility, hence the eggs and the rabbits. Passover was there too, and later tacked on to that we have the Christian festival producing an all-encompassing Easter. Fish seem to be deeply involved too.

Anyway, the Christian religion slowly grew, more as a wandering tribe, as were the Jews and, later, the Muslims.

CHAPTER 4

More about How the Three Major Religions got Started

During the Roman Empire the Romans captured large parts of the world. They didn't seem to actually care what religion the people were. They themselves didn't have a religion as such, they just worshiped various unseen gods (though they built statues to them and there was some strange lady at Delphi who was an oracle that people seemed to like).

The Picts could run around covering themselves in blue stuff and anyone else could clearly do whatever they liked (as long as they paid whatever Rome considered was due to those in power).

That said, the Emperor Hadrian did build a wall across England to keep the Picts in Scotland and out of England. It's a long wall, for sure, but not terribly high; maybe it shrunk over time. It's certainly not on the scale of the Great Wall of China.

So, if the Picts had really wanted to take over England, they'd have just jumped over it (with, as you can imagine, much yelling and screaming and plenty of blue paint).

The Picts were Celts and the original Britons. However, after being attacked by Vikings and sundry other persons, they were pushed back into Scotland and Wales. (In all honesty, the first English I really became aware of historically were known as Anglo Saxons.) So clearly, the real Britons are tucked away somewhere in the depths of Scotland or Wales.

The Roman Empire had been around from the sixth century BC but didn't start its expansive role until about the third century. A.D. The first really famous Caesar was Julius Caesar. He had a son by Cleopatra, whom he brought to Rome, which annoyed everyone and resulted in getting himself killed by Brutus and sundry other senators. It also gave Shakespeare a fabulous plotline for a particular play.

Before that the Romans were fighting all sorts of people and taking over everyone. Then there came a series of Caesars who were barking mad: Nero burnt Rome down while supposedly playing the fiddle, then there was Caligula who declared one of his horses to be a senator. (Given the decision-making power of some actual senators, maybe a horse would be a much better option than one may have guessed for Parliamentary matters!)

Mark Anthony was one of Julius Caesar's generals and he got involved with Cleopatra too and had several children with her. He managed to infuriate the rest of the senate, and - after a lot of fighting - committed suicide. I'm not sure how he did it, but Cleopatra - also suicidal - apparently held an asp to her breast, which was much more dramatic and made extremely good material for another of Shakespeare's plays. I was never entirely sure what an asp was, but discovered it is a small type of cobra. (There's also a fish - an Eurasian freshwater carp - called an asp, but somehow I don't think Cleopatra died from fish bite.)

Meanwhile, China built a wall around itself and ignored the rest of the world. In a very early-Medieval way, they were medically and scientifically hundreds of years ahead of their European neighbours, but they were also quite barbaric and had no wish to have anything to do with those whom they referred to as 'The foreign devils'. Their wall kept the world at bay (though they did trade with people who were brave enough to follow the Silk Road). However, with all their medical and scientific knowledge, they surely could have come up with something easier to eat with than chopsticks!

Basically, in history, it seems that when most people have nothing much to do in the summer, they enjoy starting wars! For once, people weren't fighting over religion. It was land and expansion that they wanted. The Christians weren't seen as a problem and were batted out of the way. The Romans used them to feed the lions as a sort of afternoon entertainment. The Jews and the Muslims (when the latter appeared around the seventh century) seemed to others to be very similar; simply wandering tribes whom they tolerated or made into slaves as the mood took whoever was in power at the time.

In the early 3rd Century AD the Emperor Constantine's mother, who was looking for something to do, came across a tribe of Jesus's followers. The idea of having just one God clearly appealed to her. She decided it was exactly what the Romans needed rather than a whole bunch of different and hard-to-remember gods. These Christians had one God (far easier to remember), and this one didn't appear to be particularity violent. So this new God seemed to incorporate everything that was needed in a religion, and Constantine's mother managed to talk her son, who had a lot of other things on his mind (and really, by the way, who wants to be arguing with their mother, especially about religion?) into becoming Christian and changing the various Roman gods into one. Thus was the beginning of the Catholic Church.

As Constantine was living in Constantinople at the time, I imagine Constantinople was named after him. However, the hub of the Catholic Church finally moved to Rome where it remains today.

Then a game changer happened at the beginning of the seventh century AD. Muhammad appeared and, although unable to read or write, got someone to write down his thoughts into what became known as The Koran. (I say his thoughts, but it was all supposedly revealed to him over some twenty-three years by the archangel Gabriel.) It was a book full of rules, with a bit of fire and brimstone thrown in just to make sure people obeyed those rules. It is considered, along with the Bible, a guide to the way a particular people should live. (Neither book, however, threatens the others' religion. There was no "Unless you become Christian/Muslim we will kill every one of you.") This then was the beginning of the faith of Islam.

CHAPTER 5

Charlemagne

Charlemagne appears to be the father of France, (which was at the time was known as "Franks" having previously been "Gaul"). He conquered Northern Italy, Germany, and Northern Spain. His father had the quaint name of 'Pepin the Short' (being a polite way of saying he was a hunch-back - but in no way related to Richard III). Still, Pepin seems an odd name for a king…it's clearly okay as a pet's name but for royalty? No.

I remember that a friend, choreographer Sammy Bayes, and I saw the musical "Pippin" when it was playing on Broadway in the early 1970s. It had nice music, and about Charlemagne and his first son, who was obviously named after his grandfather but wasn't necessarily 'short'.

As the Roman Empire crumbled, Charlemagne seems to have picked up the pieces. Fighting with everyone who got in his way, Charlemagne took over, giving people names such as "Charles the Bald" (king of what was to become France), and "Louis the German"(king of what eventually became Germany, after being a whole bunch of other places). So, not what you'd call a creative mind.

He had all kinds of battles with people I've never heard of, but he also fought with the Saxons and, naturally, the Muslims, before eventually setting up medieval Europe so that it could fight amongst itself for several hundred years to come.

CHAPTER 6

England and its Various Goings-on until Magna Carta

The Vikings invaded as did the Danes and somehow the people of England became Anglo Saxons and I don't know much about them except they all seem to have peculiar names and were kings of odd parts of England; King Alfred was King of Wessex which appears now to be in Berkshire, battled with the Danes and seems to have won and said, "Right-o, now I'm King of England," and Wessex disappeared. His other claim to fame seems to have been that he burnt some cakes near the town of - or actually in - Wantage (where he seems to have spent most of his time). My brother went to a school in Wantage, named after King Alfred. Why a king should be spending his time baking cakes in the first place, or why it's memorable, I have no idea, but apparently it is.

"Cnut" (which is Olde English, but for those who tend not to speak Olde English - most of us, really, I should think - it's spelled and pronounced as "Canute"), supposedly sat at the seashore and commanded the sea to go back. To where, I'm not sure. Ethelred another king was unready, but for what exactly, who knows?

Finally, we had William the Conqueror from Normandy, who clearly had nothing to do that particular summer of 1066 (plus he had a standing army), so he looked over the Channel at the English coast line, and said, "There's nothing much happening here, so let's invade England!".

Over he came, hit the reigning Saxon King Harold in the eye with an arrow at Hastings and thus became the new King of England. He rampaged up and down England to make everyone aware he was the new king, bringing with him large chunks of France and a few chums. He then proceeded to build the Tower of London and create this huge book called "The Domesday Book" (which offered as many unpronounceable names and words as you could ever dream of, all in the one place). In it he made a note of absolutely everything in England. (It was like a low-tech version of Google Maps and Wikipedia combined.) There are apparently particular trees mentioned in it that are still in existence. William then seems to have gone back to Normandy. When he died he left sundry sons. The eldest, William, became William II but he spent most of his time in Normandy. He was known as "Rufus", most presumably because of his red hair. When he died in a hunting accident in 1100, his brother Henry seized the throne.

Henry I was a hard man but a good manipulator, and he brought in some effective innovations to do with the justice system and the workings of government. He died without a male heir, and so there was considerable confusion as to who should reign next. There was Matilda, his daughter, and there was Stephen, his nephew, both of whom claimed their right to the throne. Although Stephen did get himself crowned, it didn't seem to stop them fighting. They spent years battling it out and most of the time Stephen won, but Matilda did have the odd victory. Things didn't calm down till Henry Plantagenet got fed up with the "I'm king/no, you're not, I'm queen" battle that seemed to have been going on for far too long, so he stepped in and said, "Oh, for God's sake, enough! Stop this, it's annoying and a terrible waste of everyone's time. I'm king!". For some odd reason this seemed to work; maybe he had more soldiers than the Saxons. He certainly was the sort of person people took notice of and all the bickering stopped and he became King.

Henry II was the son of Matilda and the grandson of Henry I. Matilda had married into the Plantagenet family, so it was the end of the Normans and the beginning of the Plantagenets, which also brought Anjou, in France, under England's wing. His wife, Eleanor of Aquitaine, had previously been married to Louis VII of France. When he suddenly died, Eleanor married Henry and brought with her Aquitaine, another French "acquisition".

The French were furious that quite large chunks of their country now seemed to belong to the English and Henry II. Not even the Pope, when he started his crusades, could stop them fighting. This continued through various royal houses, from the Plantagenets to the Lancasters, until it finally ended with England losing most of its French possessions and the death of Henry V. (Among other things that we're left with is a terrific speech Shakespeare had Henry make in his play "Henry V".) The English only really stopped fighting the French when they started fighting the Germans, but we'll talk about that much later on.

Meanwhile, back to Henry II. He was very friendly with a bishop called Thomas A'Beckett. When an opening came up, Henry made Thomas Archbishop of Canterbury, thinking that, as they were friends, Thomas would do whatever he wanted him to. Both his mother and Eleanor told Henry this wouldn't work and it didn't. Thomas took his role as archbishop very seriously, and the two of them practically came to blows about nearly everything, until one evening Henry exclaimed, "Will no one rid me of this troublesome priest?" - or words to that effect. I don't think he was really being serious as he was probably drunk at the time, but he said it in front some of his knights, who probably thought, "Right-o!", and off they went to Canterbury where they hacked poor Thomas to death. If it's any consolation, he was made a saint and (somewhat later) there was a famous play and a couple of films about it all, in one of which Anthony Hopkins broke his leg (I'll bet you didn't know that!).

Meanwhile, to say that Henry and Eleanor had a dramatic marriage would be to understate the matter. She was extremely bright, as was he, and they bickered and clashed the whole time (well, most of the time - they did manage to have eight children). Eleanor tended to side with her sons against Henry. Eventually he got so annoyed with her that he had her imprisoned. He did enjoy arguing with her, however, so they kept up an odd sort of relationship, and when he died Eleanor became regent. Henry was a great one for taking over things. He invaded Ireland, parts of Scotland and Wales, really annoying the Picts, who at this stage had stopped painting themselves blue. (Why on earth they'd done it in the first place seems weird to me. I picture them as being Smurf-like creatures!) Henry also liked collecting parts of France he didn't already have. He didn't seem to care for any of his five sons as whenever there was a family fight they all sided with their feisty mother over everything.

From their various goings on, the sons were an strange lot. Geoffrey seemed perhaps to be the least odd of them but suddenly he vanished. Upon my first forays into researching the fate of Geoffrey, I couldn't quite find out what had happened to him. I was very busy at the time with a new P.R. firm, so everyone I spoke to I asked, "What happened to Henry II's son, Geoffrey?". Finally, I was talking to a girlfriend, named Katy Pie, who had a television morning show on Channel Ten. And naturally, I asked her about Geoffrey.

"Oh, he got killed in a jousting tournament," Katy replied.

I was dumbfounded. Of all the people I thought might know anything about Geoffrey, Katy was the last person on earth I imagined would. You see, everyone knows something about history. Geoffrey did indeed, as Katy said, get himself killed in a jousting match, which was the football of its day, only it was a lot more dangerous, evidently, as it killed Geoffrey!

Europe was a feudal society, as was most of the known world. There weren't many large countries with any real power. There was no Germany, nor Italy, but there was the Holy Roman Empire and, of course, France. Russia was huge and, at that time, minding its own business, as was China. The Netherlands, though small, was a seafaring nation and really quite rich and powerful. England wasn't quite sure what it was as half its kings were French, spoke French and spent a lot of their time in France. The middle of Europe was populated by hundreds of tiny little states presided over by kings, princes and dukes, under whom were lords, barons, counts, peasants and serfs. All were beholden to whomever was above them in rank, and could be called upon to fight any time their lord and master felt like it. (They also had the most unpronounceable names!) Having what amounted to a ready-made army, there were numerous battles going on.

Every so often one of these tiny countries would feel like attacking its neighbour and seeing if it could acquire some more land. They only went to war in the summer; once it got cold, wet and muddy, they all - in a plan which sounds very sensible to me - went home and started again in the spring. Very much later, when it came to trench warfare, I can't think why they did away with the idea.

Another thing of interest about this period in history is that most of the people were basically drunk all the time. This probably caused a lot of the beheadings and other grotesque goings on. They couldn't drink water because it was putrid, so they had to drink ale. Imagine drinking booze all day long. No wonder a whole lot of very strange decisions were made!

A little earlier, Pope Urban II had looked at all these small countries fighting each other and decided the whole thing was far too disruptive. So he gathered the major kings and princes together and said, "You want to fight? I'll give you something to fight about. Get together as many allies as you can, plus of course, your own armies and go and fight the Infidel and make sure you get the Holy city of Jerusalem back!".

This seemed to appeal to everyone, because if you weren't a farmer summer was sometimes a bit boring anyway, and a good war livened thing up a bit (and would appear to please God too), so they all went gleefully off to Europe crashing and bashing around. Thus, we have the start of the (somewhat oxymoronically-titled) "Holy Wars" and, of course, "The Crusades". Also, as you may know, at around the same time the Knights Templar came to be formed.

Henry was not a popular king and not many grieved when he died. Richard the Lion Heart of England, whom Henry had reluctantly recognised as his heir after much fighting, became king. (I think Richard preferred fighting people more than actually being king.) He got himself captured by Leopold V of Austria. Heaven knows why he was captured because presumably they were on the same side. Leopold held him for a ransom that nearly bankrupted England. Richard eventually died fighting. Just read up on him and you will find people simply didn't like him. I suppose it is difficult to care for someone who says, "How do you do? Let's fight!". It seems it was all he ever wanted to do, which irritated the whole of Europe, so that was probably why King Leopold was delighted to capture him. (Also the literal "king's ransom" may have had something to do with it.)

"King John was not a good man," as A. A. Milne once said. Most of the Plantagenets had some sort of charm but King John, Richard's brother and next in line to the throne, was sadly lacking in that department. He also seemed not to have any land, which was odd for a royal prince, so was known as "Lack-land"; hardly original but that was his name. Under the impression that being king meant that he had some sort of "divine right", he taxed the people until life was unbearable. His barons got together and wrote a charter of rights and cornered him. "You read this and you sign it, or we'll chop your head off," was the essence of what they said. Realising that they probably meant it, he did! And as Marriott Edgar so quaintly put it in his poem "The Magna Carta": "In England today, you can do what you like, as long as you do what you're told." And that was the Magna Carta, signed in 1215 and the basis of all Western law today.

Apart from having to sign the Magna Carta, for some reason I honestly don't understand, John decided to take the Crown Jewels out for a road trip. Possibly, he was just being a show-off as even though nobody liked him, he still had the Crown Jewels! He was crossing the Wash, which is marshland in the Eastern part of England, and there was some sort of a storm and the whole lot were lost in the Wash, as it were. Another blot on his copybook. The Magna Carta, however, did work out well.

CHAPTER 7

More about The Knights Templar

During all the sieges of Jerusalem, many people who had nothing to do with the crusades were getting themselves killed by simply trying to visit the Holy Land. I mean, however religious you are, why would you walk into the middle of a war zone? It was not the time to decide to take a holiday in Jerusalem! I have to wonder if it was all to do with people drinking far too much ale.

So, a French knight, who also belonged to a holy order of monks, went to King Baldwin of Jerusalem (by the way, I find that a really odd name for a King of Jerusalem, and as far as I know he was no relation to Alec or any of the other more recent Baldwin tribe) and said, "My group and I are monks sworn to poverty, but we are also fighting monks, so how about we join the crusades to make sure people who are not crusaders do not get killed?".

The king liked the idea and gave them quarters in the Temple Mount. Pope Innocent II allowed them to cross borders without having to pay tax. As they were a charitable order, numerous contributions came rolling in. Then things started to change. The monk knights found they actually enjoyed fighting more than the saving people. Soon they were in the thick of the crusades, having a glorious time beating up any unfortunate infidel who happened to come their way.

They also became bankers for the various knights who went on the crusades. The knights would hand over all their money for safe-keeping to the Templars, who issued what amounted to letters of credit (and in the process became extremely rich, especially if the people who had handed the money over to them happened to die), plus they lent money. You could safely say they were the first World Bankers (and they obviously forgot their vow of poverty!).

This was fine until Philip IV of France realised how much money he owed them. He pondered what to do. He couldn't throw them out of the country because the Pope had given them the right to go anywhere they liked. In the end he did what any self-respecting king of those times would have done: he had them all killed! (Royalty was quite charming in those days; with a wave of the hand thousands died.) Ever since there have been rumours about all the Templar gold with people hunting around, trying to discover what happened to it; they assume it must be stashed somewhere. As yet, it's not been found. However, every so often someone makes a film about it.

CHAPTER 8

The Habsburgs

The Habsburg Empire was not so much a country as a group of them. It started off small as a dukedom in the early eleventh century with a tiny castle which is now in Switzerland. ("Habsburg' can also be spelt with a "P". The English like it that way, but as the Empire was named after the castle in Switzerland that they were living in, Castle Habsburg, and it is the Austrian way of spelling it, we will continue with the "B". I find it odd that the Austrian duke named himself after the house - quite different from the English who usually name the house after themselves.) As they grew, they started, shall we say, "acquiring" land, and in 1276 Rudolph of Habsburg moved their power-base to the Duchy of Austria. Over time, they grew very large indeed, incorporating Bohemia, Hungry, Slovakia, Croatia, Serbia, the Ukraine and Burgundy (which a lot of countries, including England, seemed to own at some time or another).

Poland also kept bobbing up as variously belonging to Russia, the Ottoman Empire, or the Austrians, at different points in time. From Austria's point of view, the most annoying of the various countries they sometimes had control over was Hungary; whatever anyone did with it, the Hungarians wanted to do the opposite, and Serbia was a damned nuisance as well.

Spain, being the largest country down the bottom of Europe, had been a battlefield between the Catholics and the Turks for hundreds of years and it wasn't until Catherine of Castile and Ferdinand of Aragon got together and married that they had enough power to push the Turks and the Jews out. They became part of the Habsburg Empire when their daughter Joanna married a Habsburg and her son, Charles, became the first Spanish Habsburg.

Before that, there had been a whole lot of to-ing and fro-ing on Joanna's behalf, to make sure her son did succeed to the Habsburg title; she may even have bumped off one of the other people who held title to the Spanish throne. Joanna was known as "Joanna the Mad". When her husband died she supposedly had his corpse embalmed and took it everywhere she went. She was eventually deposed as queen and declared a lunatic.

The two Habsburg empires ruled their various parts of Europe until the 1700s when the Spanish Habsburgs died out. Most of them, for quite a while, had been intermarrying and as a result were as nutty as fruitcakes. (Joanna would have felt right at home.)

At the end of the 1st World War, Austria lost its Empire, as did Russia, Germany and the Ottoman Empire, which was actually disintegrating anyway, giving Lawrence of Arabia a chance to gather the Arabs together and fight for England. (Great movie, though I did feel that David Lean could have given us a little less time staring at sand.) The Arabs had previously mainly been under the control of the Ottomans.

Then there was Russia, which tended to mind its own business, though they would occasionally leap out and grab something (usually Poland). Russia also had no interest in the rest of Europe and tended to remain quite old-fashioned in their habits, in a very early-medieval way (even after the rest of Europe had progressed and had become, in comparison, quite sophisticated).

France became interested in making grabs for parts of Europe when Louis XIV came into his own, but prior to that it had spent most of its time fighting with England. Louis XIV will keep popping up, because he lived for such a long time, through reign after reign of everyone else.

(Seventy-seven years was a grand old age for those days, and he had ascended the throne when he was four years old! But more of that later.)

The Turks were on their way to creating the Ottoman Empire which would eventually consist of the Balkans, Kosovo, Bosporus, Timor, Persia, Jerusalem, Bosnia, Moldavia, Kurdistan and parts of Georgia. You can see why Pope Urban II had been so concerned. He had tried the Crusades, but what was needed was something larger to keep the Turks from taking over the whole of Eastern Europe.

(The Holy Roman Empire with the Austrian and Spanish components came much later. That was Pope Leo III's way of dealing with the Ottoman Empire.) Both Austria and Spain were run by Habsburgs and were large enough to keep the Ottoman Empire from over-running them.

China, although very isolationist, did trade with the rest of the world. Marco Polo visited in the late 1200s and came back with noodles, which later became spaghetti. The problem was that nobody in Venice believed he had actually been to China. Though he wasn't the first European to visit China, very few had ever been there. He described the place in great detail, but they thought he was just making it up. Still, they liked the noodles.

In the early Middle Ages, the city of Venice was a great sea-trading centre. Technically, it shouldn't have actually existed, being built over a bunch of small islands covered in muddy swamp land. By feats of brilliant engineering the Venetians managed to build one of the most beautiful cities in the world. Because they had a large navy, they were a very rich, a trading nation who didn't seem to go in for a fight quite as much as everyone else did. Venice became a republic in 1697 and was ruled by various Doges, or magistrates. I don't know where I got this from but I think the Doges ran a sort of secret service, a bit like the FBI and the CIA entwined. They spied on the people, and the populace was quite frightened of them. I believe they also had an enormous torture chamber from whence few people ever came out alive. But I may have that all wrong.

Venice is a very beautiful city. One of its most famous citizens was Giacomo Casanova. He was one of only two people who managed to escape from the torture chamber in which he was held, probably for sleeping with some important person's wife.

The architecture of Venice is wonderful and it makes beautiful glassware and is also fabulously unique because it doesn't have cars, only boats, to get around.

CHAPTER 9

Just a Few Pieces of Information

About the mid-1300s the Black Plague devastated almost the entire world. It started in Asia, then made its way along the Silk Road and into Europe where it peaked from 1347 to 1351. More than 20 million Europeans died - almost one-third of the continent's population.

It seemed they'd no sooner got over that when all of a sudden everybody wanted to be Pope. There were three of them: one in Rome, one in Avignon (which apparently has a bridge that goes nowhere) and one in Pisa. How this all got sorted out I have no idea, but Rome must have won because that is where the one and only Pope lives today.

Meanwhile, the Jews were quietly living their lives anywhere that people would let them. They had absolutely no desire to turn everyone around them into Jews. They wanted one day to get back to Jerusalem because so many things were denied them. Most of them could read and write and to study was one of the few things not on the black-list. Jews love to argue, to dissect and to wonder how things came about and what the actual meaning is behind this and that. Hours are spent reading the Torah and talking about what it actually means.

This gives them very analytical minds and so they turned their attention to money. The Christians were banned by holy law from lending money for profit. In England, some of the Jews took over what appeared to be a gap in the management. This worked well if one wasn't dealing with people such as kings (who were likely to turn nasty when it dawned on them that there was no way they were ever going to be able to pay back the money they had borrowed). The most sensible thing to do from the king's point of view was to throw out all the Jews, then not only did the king not have to pay back what he owed but he inherited all the other people's debts, which he made sure were promptly paid back to him.

It was only when Oliver Cromwell came to power and realised the Jews were extremely clever at managing money and the economy that they were allowed back into England. However, there were always a few Jews in England (mainly Sephardic), who had come over from Portugal and Spain in 1492.

I became interested in Portugal because my ancestors were all kicked out of there around 1492. It seems to have been its own country since around 1095 when the then Pope announced (in one of his famous bulletins) that Philip IV was to be king of Portugal. Portugal had its share of both the Roman and Ottoman Empires having a go at it, but it survived and at one stage was one of the richest countries, being a seafaring nation that was able to trade with the world. The Portuguese didn't believe Columbus was going to find a route to India by going the way he did, so they went the other direction and did actually find India. Finally, Portugal sort of dwindled as a major nation and managed to stay out of both world wars, thus coming to be as is it is today: a jolly good place for a holiday.

All my lot seem to have been in England since the mid-1700s. Where they were before that, I haven't worked out (probably Holland as we are Sephardic). That seems to mean everyone's surname is a Christian name (pardon the expression). They had quite large families and where the surname was, say Joseph, there was almost inevitably a son named Joseph, so you got Joseph Joseph. The same with Moses, Phillip, Emanuel and so on, all of which shows a great lack of imagination (or I suppose it could be some sort of Sephardic tradition).

Our Sephardic food is very different. The first time I came across chopped liver was at a school friend's house when I was fifteen, I thought, "Where have they been hiding this? Yummy!", but I know not everyone reacts that way.

CHAPTER 10

The Hundred Years War

The French decided to do something about what they regarded as a grave injustice. There was France (a large, noble country), and England appeared to own at least half of it. Determined to get back what they felt was rightfully theirs, a major war broke out. This started around 1337, shortly after the end of the Black Death. Little did anyone know this particular war was going to go on for a hundred and sixteen years and, again, imaginatively, is quaintly known as "The Hundred Years War".

It started when Charles IV of France died. There was no male heir and the French would not allow a woman to come to the throne; all hell broke out when they realised the nearest male relative was Edward II of England. Not only did England already own lots of France, it also appeared that England wanted it all. Phillip V of the house of Valois decided he should be king and the two countries battled about it for the next hundred and sixteen years. Halfway through, Scotland and some of the French changed sides, so there were French areas such as Burgundy fighting for the English while Scotland was on the French side. The royal houses involved on the French side were Capot and Valois. The English had Angevin and Plantagenet, and, of course, everyone went home for the winter. It must have been incredibly muddling, knowing who had been where and what they'd been doing when they started again at the beginning of spring!

There were also numerous little splinter-groups engaged in smaller wars, although they probably didn't seem all that small to the people involved, such as the War of the Two Peter and the War of Portuguese Succession, which I have tried to understand but it drove me mad. Maybe it was all too logical. Unless there is a crazy person or a genius in charge, I tend to stay away from it. No wonder the whole thing lasted so long with little wars breaking out every so often and then, of course, everyone having to regroup after the winter.

The various Popes were still egging people on to go on crusades - which they did, thus avoiding whatever French and the English were doing at the time - mainly I think because the Turks and the Ottoman Empire had control of most of eastern Europe and the Popes were terrified of losing control completely. Meanwhile, the Hundred Years War was still going strong.

Joan of Arc, a young peasant girl, was in there somewhere when God apparently told her to go to war and take France back from the English. She did very well and managed to get Charles VII crowned at Reims, but then she was captured by the Burgundians who, being pro-England, burnt the poor girl at the stake. After a while the French decided this wasn't a good thing and made her a saint.

Henry V of England won a great battle at Agincourt, which no one thought was possible as he had far fewer soldiers than the French, but amazingly he did win. It had something to do with long bows and for a while the English had the upper hand and, as I said, he made a lovely speech, or rather Shakespeare did.

Obviously, over the course of a hundred and twenty years there were several English kings, many of them named Edward. One was called "Edward the Confessor". He must have been one of those people who take everything upon themselves and whatever goes wrong is naturally their fault. I suppose this was quite a useful character trait to have as far as the people were concerned; for convenience-sake when something went wrong, everyone could simply point at the king and say, "It's all his fault!". Another Edward, whom they really didn't like at all (simply because he was homosexual) was, unfortunately, slaughtered in a horrifying way. While the English kings were often named Edward, the French kings were mostly either Phillip or Louis.

One thing I will also never understand is how the various kings were under the illusion they were there by "divine right", that is, they derived their authority from God and could not be held accountable by man. It's nonsense! Even a half-drunk mad man would know, surely, that one became king either via inherited means, or by hook, or by crook (very often!), or, most popularly, by war (in which the best man's army obviously won). What's divine about that? If the monarchs had children, then they created a dynasty, all "divine", which continued until the line died out or until someone else came along with a bigger army and took over, bestowing upon themselves, along with everything else, the so-called "divine right".

CHAPTER 11

The War of the Roses

Finally, with the death of Henry V in 1422, the wretched war with France ground to a halt. However, as most of his relatives near and far wanted to take over the throne, we're straight into the War of the Roses.

England no longer had time to be bickering with the French; far better to be bickering with each other. Henry V's son Henry VI took over for a while, but then the House of York decided they should have a go at being king. John of Gaunt, who appeared to be everybody's uncle, got mixed up in it all, then the Lancastrians got in on the act. The Yorkists had white roses and the Lancastrians red.

The really memorable monarch, except for Henry V, was Yorkist Richard III, and that's because of Shakespeare! Actors love playing Richard nearly as much as Hamlet, King Lear and Macbeth. (My favourite Richard was Anthony Sher, who played him like a creepy spider.) For some reason Richard killed the two young princes in the Tower of London. Again, I have no idea why, but probably because he feared they had some "divine right" to the throne.

Finally, in 1485, there was Henry VII, who had as much right to the throne as the other two. He was related in some way to them all by his great-great-grandmother, and thought to himself, "Alright I've had enough of this. Everybody stop! I'm king!" and he was so forceful that they yielded to his wishes and he took over. However, there was probably a fight. Naturally, there would be, as nothing ever seemed to happen unless some sort of a battle took place (unless, of course, it was winter). Henry's side won, and with this, obviously, came the "divine right", meaning he could do what he liked! So now we have the House of Tudor.

Henry VII was Welsh and had nothing to do with roses whatsoever. He sorted out the country's finances, made a quite reasonable king, but was more like a book-keeper than anything else. He liked to have order and to keep the books balanced.

CHAPTER 12

Ferdinand and Isabella

Meanwhile, Spain was under the control of the Islamic Empire along with Jews and Christians, living in harmony alongside the Muslims, who had a large Empire and were living in Spain after having mainly come down from North Africa. With everyone living in accord there were some great steps taken in medicine, physics, and mathematics. Then in 1469 Ferdinand of Aragon and Isabella of Castile got married and became strong enough to take Spain away from the Muslims and the Jews. All hell broke loose. Everybody then had to be Catholic, and if they didn't want to be Catholic they were burnt at the stake.

The Inquisition, which had started in Rome around 1230, was flourishing. To avoid being converted, some Jews escaped to England and Holland. The Muslims also scattered out of the way. The Inquisition became extraordinarily popular with Catholics all over the world, terrifying those who were not Catholic, burning them to death and torturing them in the most hideous ways. Apparently, the Catholics only really stopped with their burning of heretics in the early 1800s. (Sometimes I am very puzzled by religion.)

Christopher Columbus, an Italian, set sail under the auspices of Spain to find a route to India. What he actually found were the Bahamas and on later trips, Central America. This was much better than finding India and wonderful for Spain as he came back with gold, tomatoes, potatoes, tobacco and breadfruit, all of which hadn't been seen in Europe before. Well, gold had been seen but not in the quantities Columbus was bringing home.

Over time, Spain colonised great chunks of South America, as did Portugal. England took over most of North America, apart from Louisiana, which the French got their hands on. Florida was first colonised by the Spanish in the 16th century. In the eighteenth century the English had control for about ten years, when the Spanish got it back again, until it became the 27th state of the USA in 1845. The Dutch had New York which was then called New Amsterdam. This was the era of powerful countries taking over large parts of under-developed countries, who had something the others wanted (for example, gold, cotton or tobacco), so the Americas, Africa and India were plundered.

CHAPTER 13

The Catholics, Martin Luther and Henry VIII

In Europe in the first quarter of the sixteenth century there was a growing feeling that being Catholic was a bit too over the top. With so many "heretics" being burnt to death and tortured everywhere one looked, people began to wonder if there was a religion that was not quite so hysterical and histrionic. Martin Luther and his friends started thinking that to be a Christian you shouldn't have to be quite so noisy, flamboyant, or indeed, barbaric. The movement was quietly spreading through Europe.

The Pope kept issuing Papal Bulls, which appear to be notices stuck up all over the place declaring that Martin Luther was ex-communicated along with a great many other people the Pope didn't care for (including Henry VIII). I don't know what sort of effect the Pope thought this was going to have on people who couldn't read, and the whole thing was probably in Latin anyway.

Back in England Henry VII's son, Henry VIII, was by that stage, king. He basically decided to have a flamboyant, courtly contest with the King of France, Francis I. It was given the delightfully camp name "The Field of the Clothe of Gold", and was held at Calais in France, which England happened to have "acquired" at some point or other.

It was all terribly grand with each country trying to outdo the other, with great tents, enormous feasts, beautiful clothes and jousting sessions. This was all presented as a sign of how much they loved each other and how much they wanted to live in peace. No one of note appears to have been killed. It cost an absolute fortune (all that gold clothe?) and came to nothing because almost as soon as they got home, they were at each other's throats again.

Henry decided he wanted to marry Anne Boleyn, which somewhat annoyed his present wife, Catherine of Aragon, who had given him a daughter and had had many miscarriages but who Henry felt was, by then, too old to produce a male heir. He applied to the Pope for an annulment of his marriage. The Pope wasn't about to even think about that. Catherine's father was Ferdinand (of "Ferdinand and Isabella" fame) who was doing such a good job turning everyone in sight Catholic, so the Pope wasn't going to upset him.

Henry ranted and raved and behaved like a small child. He took Hampton Court away from Cardinal Wolseley, who he felt had failed him in securing the annulment. Eventually, one of his ministers, Thomas Cromwell, came up with the bright idea that there was really no reason Henry couldn't be the head of something which they decided to call "The Church of England", and therefore perhaps didn't really need the Pope's blessing for a divorce.

Henry really liked this plan; not only could he be free to marry Anne Boleyn, but upon looking into the matter he discovered the Catholic Church was enormously wealthy, so he went around closing down monasteries and abbeys all over the place and collecting for himself the monies usually paid to the church. So, out of a combination of Henry's desire to get his own way about ending his marriage and his monetary greed, in 1534 the Church of England was spawned.

One thing he hadn't thought about was the religious side of things. He was quite happy being a Catholic, but only his sort of Catholic, which meant no more kowtowing to the Pope. Meanwhile, Martin Luther's new form of Protestant Christianity had found a way in.

Henry's main aim after he married Anne Boleyn was to have a son and heir. Anne produced a girl, Elizabeth, and then, unfortunately for her, Henry fell from his horse while jousting and the horse fell on him, leaving him with a permanently damaged leg. Whatever his doctors did to it, it never healed properly (and they did some quite ghastly things like trying to burn the sore away with a red-hot poker). From then on Henry was in incredible pain and what had been a fairly benign human being, who had once loved poetry and composed music, turned into a hideous tyrant. (Michael Flanders and Donald Swann said he wrote "Greensleeves". However, a friend of mine says he didn't and that the song existed long before Henry. I prefer to believe Flanders and Swann. It would be nice to think he had a kinder, sweeter side instead of the monster most people think him to be. My friend snorted and said "Right, the sensitive wife-killer!").

Anne became pregnant again but the child, a boy, was stillborn. Henry had a complete meltdown and had Anne and several of her friends and family beheaded (except for the Duke of Norfolk, who was Anne's Uncle and who had heavily promoted the marriage, but…more about him later).

True to his "I'm king" insistence, Henry then married Jane Seymour. She comes across as a fairly pretty, mousy little girl, but she did manage to have a son. Then she died (possibly, in retrospect, a very wise move).

Henry (while still looking for more children), married Anne of Cleves, sight-unseen, which was clearly very risky. When he did see her, he thought she looked like a horse. As Henry, even in one of his more manic moods, could not behead her for that, he divorced her instead - after six months of marriage - and from then on referred to her as "sister", which, in all consideration, was, while creepy, probably a great deal safer than being "wife".

Meanwhile, he'd noticed one of her ladies-in-waiting, Catherine Howard (who was a teenager and rather silly). Despite being in love with Francis Dereham, she married Henry - who was nearly fifty years old - and, of course, it all ended in tears with many people being beheaded, including Catherine; Frances Dereham was even hung, drawn and quartered (which is obviously a much ghastlier way to go).

By this time Henry was not feeling at all well and needed someone to look after him. His eye fell on a widow, Catherine Parr. The last thing she wanted was to marry Henry VIII as she was in love with Thomas Seymour, the brother of Jane. (Clearly, Catherine Parr was older and wiser than poor Catherine Howard.) Because Jane had produced a son, the Seymour's star blazed high in the sky and they could virtually do no wrong, but this still didn't save Catherine. When Henry wanted something, woe betide anyone who got in his way. So poor Catherine reluctantly married him. She was terrified and with good reason as no one ever knew what Henry was likely to do from one moment to the next (also, she was secretly a Protestant). All in all, she lived in dread for her life. Her main job as Henry's wife seems to have been to bandage his ulcerated leg (which, let's face it, would have smelled disgusting). When he eventually died, Catherine sighed with relief and married Thomas Seymour. He became power-hungry and got himself into all kinds of strife, endangering Elizabeth, as he and Catherine were her guardians. He was one of those people who can't help themselves as trouble naturally attracts them. There was talk that he may have molested Elizabeth - with Catherine's consent! Were they drunk at the time or paedophiles - or was it all just gossip?

Things came to a head when Thomas shot young Edward's dog. Edward, who was by that time king, took a very dim view of this, along with a whole lot of other plots and plans in which Seymour was involved. He was promptly beheaded too. As I said before, people did tend to get their heads chopped off for the oddest reasons. The caveat then is clearly: Don't shoot someone's dogs (especially if you're not sure how much the dog-owner has had to drink - or if he happens to be a hot-tempered king!).

CHAPTER 14

The Muslims, Martin Luther and Bloody Mary

Meanwhile, the Turks and their Ottoman Empire hadn't taken too kindly at having their brethren thrown out of Spain. The Muslims decided that, as the Ottomans had a very big empire, it was very insulting to be turfed out of Spain because they wouldn't become Catholic. They brooded about this for some time and began to ask "Why is it so important for everyone to be a Catholic?". In fact, if it came to that, why shouldn't everyone be Muslim? They already regarded those who weren't of the Islamic faith as "infidels" and always had done. However, they hadn't actually considered killing every infidel they met (unless they were at war with them). They thought about this and wrote the second book of The Koran as a sort of codicil to the first, only this one contained no sweetness and light. Instead, it was very angry, stating firmly that if you were not a Muslim, you were an infidel and should be killed! What had been a benign and progressive religion, living in harmony with others, started to change. No religion, whether it be Catholic or Muslim, or anything else, has the right to demand everybody do it their way. More harm has been done by various religions beating their breasts and screaming that they are right and everyone else is wrong. In fact, more wars have been instigated on their behalf than any other cause.

However, the Protestant faith was catching on in England in a big way. When Henry VIII died and his nine-year-old son came to the throne as Edward VI, his family on his mother's side, the Seymours, were very much fans of the new religion (probably because it allowed people to divorce any time they wanted to), and they promoted it. Edward died when he was sixteen and the Seymours proclaimed that Lady Jane Grey, a granddaughter of Henry VII, should be queen as she was a Protestant rather than Mary, Henry's elder daughter, who was a Catholic. People were looking at what was happening in Spain and were beginning to be not that keen on Catholics. However, England was still basically a Catholic country though the Protestant religion was catching on fast.

Lady Jane's reign as queen lasted only nine days and then the poor girl was beheaded, and Mary came to the throne. Mary, to say the least, was a trifle unhinged. She was furious that her father had divorced her mother, Catherine of Aragon, and caused the subsequent upheaval in religion and everyone's life. Her response to this was to demand everyone immediately revert to being Catholic. This, of course, wasn't about to happen. and there were major beheadings, burnings at the stake and general unpleasantness. The people called her "Bloody Mary". (In the 1920s a cocktail was named after her. You never know what life has in store. One day an unpopular queen, next a popular drink.)

Mary married Phillip II of Spain and then had the world's longest pregnancy (something like eighteen months). Of course, it was a phantom pregnancy. Phillip was embarrassed and furious and went back to Spain.

By Mary's time, there was not much left of France that England owned, so - before he left - Phillip persuaded her into battle against the French and they lost Calais. Mary was devastated, but she still went on beheading people and generally behaving in such an uncivilised and somewhat hysterical manner that it even unnerved some of the Catholics. Everyone gave a sigh of relief when she finally died as there is just so much upheaval anyone can bear. The feeling seemed to be, "Let's all be quiet and see what Elizabeth comes up with."

CHAPTER 15

Elizabeth

Elizabeth was another matter altogether. She had been brought up by the Seymour's and was a Protestant. She also spent a great deal of her young life in fear. At one stage, Mary had her locked up in the Tower of London and she never knew from one day to the next what Mary was about to do to her. So, when she came to the throne (in 1558) she was very pragmatic and her plan of campaign was "When in doubt, do nothing."

It is believed she was in love with Robert Dudley, the Earl of Leicester. She spent much of her childhood with him, including when they were locked up in the Tower together. However, her policy of "when in doubt, do nothing" irritated him and when she tried to marry him off to Mary Queen of Scots his nose got really put out of joint and he married Amy Robsart. But when poor Amy fell down the stairs and died, Robert clung on to the hope that Elizabeth might yet marry him. Did Amy fall or was she pushed? This was the question. A court case exonerated him but as far as Elizabeth was concerned there was no way she could marry him after that. The palace had far too many stairs!

I've recently seen a film about Mary Queen of Scots in which an African man features prominently in Elizabeth's court. However, in my other research on the matter, in which I've checked the official listings of all her courtiers, there's not an African or person of any ethnicity other than Caucasian in sight. I've come to the conclusion that the reason people sometimes get muddled with their historical facts is that the screenwriters or directors of historical movies often simply choose to add all kinds of extra details and bits and bobs of their own, usually with no historical foundation whatsoever (and probably just to make it more dramatic, or - as in this case - to be more politically correct). Looking at this particular film, they took several liberties. One major one, for instance, is that Elizabeth and Mary have a face-to-face confrontation. That never happened! They never met. And believe me Marry Queen of Scots' life was quite dramatic enough without needing to be livened up any further.

One thing Elizabeth did was to collect pirates! As a seafaring nation and an island, England always had a love affair with the sea and had a terrific navy. Between them Francis Drake and Walter Raleigh made a habit of attacking Spanish galleons, which were usually filled with gold on their way home from South America to Spain. Drake and Raleigh spent their time capturing them and bringing the loot back to a grateful Queen. She had never actually ordered them to do this but was very pleased that they did. They annoyed the Spanish so much that Phillip II sent a great armada to squash England once and for all, but there was a terrible gale and half the armada ended up wrecked on the coast of Ireland, and Drake demolished the rest.

Elizabeth sent Drake on a trip round the world and he became only the second person to circumnavigate the globe, Magellan being the first.

Raleigh, she really liked. He made a great fuss of her and laid his cloak down over a puddle so she wouldn't get her feet wet. I mean, who wouldn't like that? He then went off to North America and came back with tobacco.

While England was exploring North America and claiming it for itself, it also took an interest in acquiring as much of Canada as it could lay its hands on. The French had the same idea and they battled ferociously with the English over Canada. However, that was quite normal. If the English and the French weren't fighting over one thing, it was another.

Elizabeth's reign was the golden era of theatre and literature, with Shakespeare, John Donne, Ben Johnson and Francis Bacon (who, while I was a schoolgirl and wanting to be different, I was convinced wrote most of Shakespeare's stuff. However, he obviously couldn't have done so as he got himself killed in a tavern brawl fairly early on in the piece).

Slowly, as the English began to colonise North America, they began to realise they could grow cotton and tobacco there, capturing and indenturing slaves as part of their plan. They also took over Canada, but all I can remember about that from school was that General Wolfe climbed up a wall or a cliff or something and captured Quebec from the French, but Quebec to this day remains a very French city, so I don't know what he actually achieved.

Later, all the Scottish Highlanders left for Canada after Butcher Cumberland had decimated the Highlands of Scotland. I don't really know much about Canada, except that they play terrific ice hockey.

Elizabeth straddled the Protestants and the Catholics and tried to keep everyone from murdering each other, but she had a problem: Mary Queen of Scots was next in line to the English throne and she was a Catholic.

In Italy, about this time Galileo popped up. I've tried reading about him and I know we simply must have learnt about him in school. He probably wasn't odd enough for me. I tend to get interested in people who either do peculiar things or are naturally odd or brilliant. I'm quite sure Galileo was brilliant, but I, as I quite often do, missed the point. He was an astronomer and kept coming up with theories, which annoyed the contemporary Pope who had him arrested. It had something to do with whether the world was round and the moon had anything to do with tides, when of course everyone knew that God organised everything including the moon and the tides. I don't know how seriously he was taken during his life time, though according to Einstein some of his ideas were excellent, yet, unfortunately, before their time.

CHAPTER 16

Mary Queen of Scots

Mary Queen of Scots' life was like a medieval soap opera. As I said, she's one of those people I find really fascinating. She was the daughter of James V of Scotland; his mother was Henry VIII's sister, Margaret. James died fairly early leaving his then wife, who was French, to become regent. She arranged a match between the dauphin of France and Mary, who was sent over to France to get used to the court and marry the dauphin. That's exactly what she did, and was eventually crowned Queen of France.

The French took this opportunity to declare not only was she Queen of France and of Scotland, but also Queen of England. This pissed the English off no end. However, she was Queen of France for only about ten minutes before Francis died. Now surplus to requirements in France, they said, "You're Queen of Scotland so go and rule them!", and sent her home. The problem was that she had been brought up as a Catholic, and Scotland was by then rampantly Scottish Presbyterian (and there is nothing more rampant than a Scottish Presbyterian!).

Elizabeth tolerated her but became irritated when word got back to her that Mary was considered far prettier than she was. It must have been a very stupid person who told Elizabeth that. Pragmatic she may have been, but she was definitely vain. She was even more put out when later on Mary had a baby, and a male at that.

For a while Mary was guided by her half-brother, the Earl of Moray, but she still kept leaning towards Catholicism. Elizabeth watched from England and decided something should be done to try to calm everything down. So, she sent one of her chief ministers, William Cecil, (who later became the 1st Baron Burghley, and one of the great-grandfathers of Jonathan Cecil, a friend of mine) to sort things out.

Meanwhile, John Knox (who was one of those unbelievably religious people, a Scottish Presbyterian to a point of it being extremely irritating to everyone, not only the Queen) appeared on the scene. (Knox was played by David Tennant in a film I saw about Mary Queen of Scots. Honestly, I'd never have recognised David Tennant in this role in a thousand years as he appeared complete with an enormous beard and looking very straggly.)

Knox's main claim to fame (apart from roaring endlessly at Mary) was to denounce both Mary and Queen Elizabeth as "a monstrous regiment of women". This elaborate insult has, since then, given numerous writers a great title for their various books. Knox was sort of like an early version of the American "Holy Rollers". Well, of course he got stuck into Mary immediately, nagging at her, threatening all kinds of doom and gloom. Till Mary said, "Will you go away? I am Queen; you are annoying me, and you smell. Shoo!" The trouble was of course, he didn't.

William Cecil was a diplomatic man but he was a worrier. England was basically the only Protestant game in town and he worried about Catholic plots, though I still think that the Spanish Armada had more to do with Elizabeth's ships pinching Spanish gold than a Catholic plot. Cecil organised a spy ring lead by Francis Walsingham, with code breakers rather like an early mini version of Bletchley. Of course, when Mary landed in Scotland it was a sign for every Catholic in town to come up with a plan to dethrone Elizabeth and put Mary in her place.

Mary was, by that point having spent her early life in France, very French and feminine, positively girly, the very opposite of Elizabeth. They ended up with an agreement that she should marry Lord Henry

Darnley. This worked well for a while and they had a son, James, but Darnley had delusions of grandeur and wanted to be more than a consort. He wanted to be king and launched all kinds of plots and became something of a bloody nuisance himself.

Meanwhile, Mary had met James Hepburn, the Earl of Bothwell, who was much more to her liking. For some reason that I've never quite understood, Darley killed David Rizzo, Mary's secretary, in front of her. (In the film it's something to do with him being homosexual and the whole court was involved in killing him.) I've actually been on a sightseeing trip and having stood in the actual room in which this very event is said to have unfolded. Let me tell you, that actual room is very, very small (so yet again, the film director's imagination had run wild by supposing it was a large enough space to hold a large, shocked crowd, but hey, that's showbiz for you!). There was no way everybody would have fitted in let alone managed the mass mayhem of the film in that small room; it would have turned into total chaos and everyone would have ended up dead. So, I'm pretty sure it was just Darnley who killed the poor man. Well, that was it; he had to go, and so Bothwell blew him up. I mean, naturally that's the sort of thing one would do, don't you think? Then there was major mayhem, much running around and Bothwell is supposed to have also raped Mary. Truly chilling stuff, indeed. (But one wonders if rape was necessary as Mary was rather keen.) Anyway, they got married and they were on the run - Mary at the time being pregnant with twins (she later miscarried) - charging round Scotland being pursued by a very cross Earl of Moray, who took charge of Mary's son, James. Finally, Mary ended up in England, demanding that Elizabeth help her as she was next in line to the English throne.

As she was a Catholic, none of Elizabeth's ministers were too keen on having her around, but of course all the Catholics in England were. Elizabeth confined her in various castles, until, after nineteen years in captivity with virtually a new plot every six months or so, Elizabeth and her advisors were all getting older and tired and had had enough of Mary. It ended up with a lot of people having their heads chopped off including the Duke of Norfolk. Elizabeth, whose rule to live by had always been "When in doubt, do nothing" was suddenly confronted with the problem of needing to cut off of a royal personage's head, just to keep the peace and to keep everything from escalating. She instead had a right royal tantrum herself and banished William Cecil, which didn't really matter because he had a son, Robert, who was as smart, if not smarter than, his father and took over the reins smoothly.

I'm very impressed with the various Dukes of Norfolk (even though their family was Catholic). And occasionally, even if one of them got their heads chopped off, they somehow always seems to get themselves reinstated. The Elizabethan Norfolk seemed to be involved in plotting up to his neck, so Elizabeth did chop that particular duke's head off, but Charles II reinstated the title, so it was alright in the end (though the one who lost his head might not agree).

Today, the present Duke of Norfolk is the premier Catholic peer and organises all the major grand events such as coronations, and has the odd title of "The Queen's Butler" (which, let's face it, is very strange!).

But I digress. In the end it got to be so ridiculous and time-consuming with Mary, her various admirers and their plots, that Elizabeth finally had to behead her. She did so very sadly.

Meanwhile, Elizabeth amused herself pretending she might marry all sorts of foreign princes who arrived to woo her, but in the end she always backed out. I have no idea why she never married (although there are many theories about why this is so). Once Mary's son, James, was born and being brought up as a Protestant the line of succession appeared to be okay.

Elizabeth really was a wise Queen and managed to keep things on an even keel for most of her reign. When she died it was the end of the Tudors and the beginning of the Stuarts' reign.

CHAPTER 17

James I of England and VI of Scotland

James VI of Scotland was Mary Queen of Scots' son. He succeeded Elizabeth and became James I, king of England, in 1603. Compared to the rest of his family he was quite boring, but most people liked him because he seemed fairly harmless. He spent his time bickering with the Scots clans and their various factions as to whether they were part of England or were still Scotland. He didn't appear to be interested in fighting with France, so there was relative peace and they saved money (wars are so expensive). It was left up to Robert Cecil, William Cecil's son (and Jonathan Cecil's ancestor), to run the country. James did have the Bible translated into English from the Hebrew and Greek, but as very few people could read, I don't suppose it made a great difference to most lives. James also chopped off Sir Walter Raleigh's head for conspiring against him. This didn't go down at all well with the populous.

A couple of people tried to blow him up. The most famous of these was Guy Fawkes, whose plan was to blow up the Houses of Parliament. In England today, the Fifth of November (incidentally, my sister's birthday) is still celebrated with bonfires and "Guys", which are effigies of Mr. Fawkes, and fireworks. People outside England find it most odd that the English celebrate with relish the fact that someone tried to blow up Parliament.

Then along came the Thirty Year War. This was started by the Austrian emperor Ferdinand II who came to the throne in 1619 and was the first emperor to be educated by the Jesuits, whom everyone seems to thinks of as being a bit tricky. I'm not terribly sure why. However, even today, if one says, "Oh, he's been brought up by the Jesuits", people nod wisely and tend to say things like "Ah!".

The Jesuit tradition is very academic and offers students the option to develop the ability to truly think for themselves. I guess you could say it's the thinking person's ideal type of religious education.

Ferdinand was horrified to discover that Martin Luther had been going around turning many of his subjects into Protestants and the entire war appeared to be about who wanted to be Catholic and who wanted to be Protestant. England even got dragged into it because James I's daughter, Elizabeth, was married to an Austrian. You'd think it wouldn't take them thirty years to decide which religion they'd like to be.

All of a sudden what started off as a sort of holy war end up being something of a grab for land with the whole of Europe involved. Austria came out of it worst because it lost a lot of territory to Russia and Prussia (which sounds like some sort of tag team). Although the whole thing went on for so long everyone else came out of it with more or less what they started with. The Netherlands gained independence from Spain, Sweden controlled the Baltic and France wasn't really satisfied, but when was it ever?

CHAPTER 18

Charles I, the Civil War, Oliver Cromwell and Tulips

When James died, his son Charles I came to the throne. He had been brought up a Protestant but had very Catholic leanings. He didn't have the same temperament as his father; he was one of those people who, despite what they've been told, still think they can do what they like and it will be all right anyway. After all, he had this 'divine right', didn't he?

He married a very Catholic wife who had such a huge influence on him that before he knew what had happened, he had involved himself, his family and his supporters in a very bloody civil war. So, he really didn't have time to get involved with the Thirty Years War, although he did lend Louis XIV some ships. As they say in "1066 and All That", "The Royalists were romantic but wrong and the Roundheads were revolting but right!" And, it tore England apart.

The Royalists had a fairly flash army but the Ironsides, as the Roundheads' troops were called, were very well trained and much more military minded. Prince Charles went on the run and hid in an oak tree (that is supposed to still exist). Eventually the Roundheads won and they cut off poor Charles I's head. And the rest of the family fled to France. So much for the divine right of Kings!

Then we got Oliver Cromwell as Lord Protector of England. In theory, he was exactly what England needed after all the upheavals with Protestants and Catholics. He was calm and had the mentality of a chartered accountant, but he leaned much more to the puritanical side of things with everyone sternly encouraged to wear black and white. There was no dancing, he shut down the theatres, drinking was banned and any kind of frivolity, so England became a very dreary place to live. However, he ran the country very well and welcomed the Jews back to help with the finances. He was very hard on the Catholics, taking away all their privileges.

A bunch of pilgrims decided they would prefer to live in America, so they set sail on the "Mayflower". They ended up in Plymouth, Massachusetts, where some Native American Indians gave them a turkey and thus began the tradition of Thanksgiving. It had always been a feast to celebrate the harvest, but the Americans made it into a much bigger affair and today whole families get together to eat turkey, watch football games, and quarrel as only families can.

With Oliver Cromwell and the puritanical way of life, we acquired witches in a big way. Anything that went wrong with a harvest, cattle dying, or money problems, was said to be a witch's fault. Suddenly witches were popping up everywhere and a sort of mass hysteria swept around the world. Little old ladies, who for years had been revered for making pills and potions to cure all kinds of ills, were now being hunted to the ground. The very simple method of discovering if someone was a witch or not was to use a thing called a dunking stool. They would sit the accused on the stool over a local pond and dunk her. If she floated, she was obviously a witch; if she sank to the bottom, she wasn't. Either way the poor women ended up dead. The alternative to the dunking stool was to torture the poor souls until they would confess to anything, and would then often be executed.

England had always had a Parliament, but it basically went along with what the king wanted in most things. This of course came more or less to an end with Cromwell, who organised an upper and a lower house. The upper house was for lords and the lower one for the plebs. You were allowed to vote if you owned a house with a hearth to cook things in! Slowly, under the Hanoverians (who couldn't speak English), Parliament took over and started making the major decisions.

England actually had liked being jolly. The people had liked to dance and drink and go to the theatre. There was not much they could do about Oliver himself, he was such a paragon of virtue, but when he died and his son was about to take over, some of the people who still had power began negotiations with Charles II: "All is forgiven, please come home. P.S.: you have to be a Protestant!". Charles, who was broke and tired of being a hanger-on in the French court, said that of course he would!

In between all this fighting and religious mayhem, people became interested in tulips. This flower had been around for years and was originally from Persia. Vienna had beautiful tulip gardens and then someone had the bright idea to introduce them into Holland although many people doubted that they would actually grow there because of the weather. But they did, and suddenly everyone started buying and selling tulips. They thought this was all great fun and it became known as "Tulip Mania". The public discovered they could get all different kinds and colours and the prices went up and up. They bought and sold bulbs at such prices that people began to use them as currency (which to me sounds daft!). Currency has to be something solid like gold, not a plant that can wither away and die if you keep it too long. Eventually, the whole thing collapsed and lots of people lost oodles of money. It was probably the first economic bubble.

CHAPTER 19

Louis XIV

In France, meanwhile, Louis XIV was coming into his own. He came to the throne when he was five and reigned for seventy-two years. During his childhood his mother, Anne of Austria, acted as regent, assisted by Cardinal Mazarin. Louis's younger days were taken up between wars with various noblemen, who felt they should be king, and the Huguenots, who revolted every so often.

Europe at that stage was divided into two lots of Habsburgs, who ruled Spain in the southern part of Europe and Austria with its empire at the top in the eastern part. Both had large empires. Russia was also there but tended to keep to itself with the occasional foray to grab a little something. France, located just above Spain, still liked to fight with England. Then there was Italy, which consisted of several small principalities. There was also Prussia, Bavaria, a number of German principalities and dukedoms (with quite unpronounceable names), Italy, which figured as mainly small principalities, and Russia and Poland. The Netherlands, Holland and Sweden appear to have stayed out of most of the European tussles. But let's not forget the Turks and their Ottoman Empire, consisting of the Balkans, Kosovo, Persia, Jerusalem, Belgrade, Bosnia, Kurdistan and parts of Georgia. Everyone was frightened of them because they were so huge and quite aggressive. So, there was a great choice if you felt like having a war.

Charles II of England had spent long periods of his life in France after the English had chopped off his father's head, and because his sister Henrietta was married to Louis XIV's brother, Philippe, there was now a truce between the two countries, a very rare occurrence as England and France were at war for most of the Middle Ages. The reason for the marriage I will get to later on. France was for ever trying to get back parts of it that for one reason or another were still under England's control.

Initially, Louis had been too busy fighting off enemies from within to worry about what England or Europe were doing. There were uprisings and plots. The Edict of Nantes, which basically said "Leave the Huguenots alone; they're not hurting anyone!", had been signed about a hundred years before Louis came to the throne and sometimes it was adhered to and sometimes it wasn't. With the Huguenots being the French version of the English Protestant, this was adhered to while Anne and Cardinal Mazarin were in control. When Louis came of age, he decided the Huguenots had to go because of their Protestantism. He began to pick on them. They were mainly spinners and weavers, and they tended to flee to Spitalfields in London, where they continued to weave their silk by hand as they had always done. They didn't want anything to do with the industrial revolution. People clearly liked their silk weaving, so why spoil a good thing?

Louis also didn't like homosexuals and wanted to ban them from France. It was then the fashion to dress young boys as girls, and as they grew older there was a "breaching ceremony" where they got trousers. However, Louis's brother, Philippe, took the whole thing a bit too far and enjoyed prancing about in ladies' clothes a great deal of the time, long after his "breaching ceremony". When Louis brought his idea of throwing all the homosexuals out of France, it was suggested to him, tactfully, that he should take a look at his brother. Philippe was swiftly married off to Henrietta, Charles II's sister. They even had children.

In the meantime, Louis was having trouble with the nobility, who were always plotting and planning various horrors. He then decided the answer was to build a very, very big house and have everyone come and live with him, so he could keep an eye on them all. If they didn't agree he just went and burnt their houses down.

A lot of Louis's time was taken up building Versailles (the very big house). It was only after he got everyone settled in where he could see them that he began looking further afield. Basically, he was an expansionist and wanted to get as much of Europe as he could under French control. This meant more fighting with England to get back the parts of France they had.

CHAPTER 20

The Devil's Number

All of a sudden it was 1666, the Devil's number, and everyone was scared witless. With all these witches around, what was going to happen? I don't know what happened in the rest of the world, but in London in 1665 a great plague swept through, brought by rats from the ships bringing goods from all parts of the world. They had just about got over that when there was the Great Fire of London, which in an odd sort of way was a good thing as it got rid of the vermin-infested conditions people were living in and they had to rebuild London. Christopher Wren rebuilt St. Paul's and a few other churches.

Nobody took the fire seriously at first, because most of the houses were made of wood, fires were always breaking out, and London's mayor practically ignored it. It was only when the king and his brother, James, took matters over and directed the fire-fighting that it was brought under control.

I think Charles II was a comparatively nice man, if not a faithful one in the marital department. Although his wife, Catherine of Braganza, was unable to produce a living heir it didn't occur to him to divorce or behead her; he was quite happy to be married as long as he could hop in and out of bed with any pretty female in sight. One of the most famous was Nell Gwynn, the Covent Garden actress. Charles genuinely liked women, especially if they were pretty and entertaining, as Nell apparently was.

[A piece of trivia: Bombay, which it was known as back then, came under British control as part of the dowry of Catherine on her marriage to Charles II. He then sold it on to the British East India Company for ten pounds a year.]

One of the first things Charles did on becoming king was to start up theatre again and set up his own troupe, the King's Players. What's not to like about that? Far better than tormenting Muslims, Jews, Huguenots, Protestants or Catholics. He was also very pragmatic. Louis XIV sent Charles's sister Henrietta over to negotiate a treaty that France would give England money if they joined together against William of Orange. "What a good idea," said Charles, who had only a few months earlier betrothed his niece Mary to said William. Against all advice James, Charles's brother, had married Anne Hyde, the daughter of one of Charles's ministers. It was a happy marriage and Anne had several children, two of whom survived, Mary and Anne, and were brought up as Protestants.

So, now there was a burgeoning variety of Christians, Protestants, Baptists, Quakers, Congregationalists, Presbyterians, Anglicans, Methodists and, of course, the Catholics, all with their different slants on Christianity. Most took it upon themselves to send missionaries off to the various colonies to teach the locals what it was to be "a good Christian". Some of them even got eaten for their pains.

Another thing Charles did was to pries New Amsterdam away from the Dutch, and thus New Amsterdam became New York and part of the English colony. When everybody wasn't beating each other up, it was a period of great learning, with theatre and all manner of interesting things occurring. Sir Isaac Newton supposedly had an apple fall on his head and he discovered gravity. He also invented the Cat Flap! Was there anything this man couldn't do? It seems he must have liked cats, a definite plus! Samuel Pepys, who was on the board of the navy, kept a diary about everything that was happening and as he was in the middle of most things, and quite a nosy-parker. It makes fascinating reading even today.

Samuel Johnson took years and years to come up with the complete dictionary of the English language. He had a chum, James Boswell, who followed him around like a puppy and if you would like to find out much more about him and some of the fascinating situations he got himself into, you must read my friend Patrick Edgeworth's play "Boswell for the Defense".

There's a comic poem that went the round during this time:
"We have a pretty King
Whose word no man relies on,
He never said a foolish thing,
And never did a wise one."

The king took it all in good part; all he really wanted was to not rock the boat. He was basically into having a quiet life and lots of pretty ladies around him. He managed to battle his way through various plots and King Louis sniping at him when he realised Charles's promises were not necessarily to be believed. When he eventually died it was as a Catholic, but I suppose he felt it was a case of asking the rhetorical question, "Who cares at this point?" Charles warned his brother before he died not to make waves, the country did not want to be Catholic. Charles's death left his brother James to become king as James II. By then, of course, Scotland had got over demanding that he be James VI.

Meanwhile, the Ottoman Empire had long been wanting to get its paws on Vienna to provide access to the Danube. It had tried and failed before, but in 1682 felt the time was right as plague had been raging in Vienna, but by the time the Ottomans got their troops together it was September and the three months they needed to get to Vienna would take them into winter. They returned in March and forged towards Vienna. The plan was to starve the Viennese out as they were already weakened by the plague. When Louis XIV refused to help, in came King John III Sobiesk, King of Poland (in one of the periods in which Poland had its own king) at the head of an army consisting of the Lithuanians and the Holy Roman Empire and saved the day, much to the annoyance of the Turks. There is a lovely statue of him in Vienna.

I feel very sorry for Poland. It was forever being divided up between Austria, Prussia and Russia, or having kings thrust upon it. The poor place didn't seem to have much of a say in what happened to it. I met a Polish prince once and, because my surname name is "Kavalek" (which means "piece" in Polish!), he assumed I must be Polish. He was very sweet and took me out a couple of times and told me his full name was "Prince Peter" and then something very Polish.

CHAPTER 21

James II

There are some people who are totally immune to good advice and James was one of those people. He ignored his brother's advice completely. While he was married to his first wife Anne Hyde (with whom he had two daughters, both firmly Protestant), he did keep to the straight and narrow to a degree, but once she had died, James married the very Catholic Mary of Modena. He seems to be a person who knows how he's supposed to behave, but still thought that though everyone was telling him to stop all this wavering towards Catholicism and keeps things as they were, he could just ignore all that and go steaming ahead and it would come out all right in the end. Really! I know people don't seem to learn from past history, but they'd only just chopped his father's head off!! What was he thinking?

Then the Duke of Monmouth (the illegitimate son of Charles II) lost his head and rose up, declaring he would make a far better king than his uncle. As a result he lost his head, literally.

If you were on trial around this era, God help you if you faced Judge George Jeffreys as he was as likely to hang you as look at you. After the Monmouth rebellion he went around the country presiding over the various trials, and it is said that he had about 1,380 people hanged. These trials were called "The Bloody Assizes". Jeffreys was very cavalier about the whole thing. He had one woman, Alice Lisle, hanged for harbouring some people who hadn't even been tried. Whether or not it was because people were terrified in case he'd hang them, but he actually had an incredibly successful career, rising to the position of Lord Chancellor and sometimes serving as Lord High Steward.

About this time John Churchill came into play. He was a fascinating character and nearly as bad as Charles II for hopping in and out of women's beds. He happened also to be an extremely good soldier and squashed the Monmouth rebellion.

By this time the country was in a real stew. If there was a wrong way to do anything, James would find it and leap in feet first. He was handing out top jobs to all his Catholic chums, though Cromwell had banned them from doing practically anything. England had had enough of Catholic kings and thought they had made it plain to James what would happen to anyone thinking it was a good idea to become a Catholic monarch. There was a major rebellion and William of Orange (who was married to Mary, James's eldest daughter) was asked by Churchill and a group of parliamentarians to come and take over the mess James was so busily creating. He said he would, but he wanted to be king and not some consul. As he seemed quite sensible and didn't appear to want to chop anyone's head off, it was decided upon. So over he came with his army with John Churchill at the helm, and James and Mary of Modena had to flee. Mary was expecting a baby, which caused all sorts of trouble later on. There were numerous rumours that the baby wasn't hers. The story went that he had been smuggled in, in a warming pan! Although their son was Catholic, he actually was, nonetheless, the rightful heir to throne.

CHAPTER 22

William and Mary

King William accepted Churchill's offer of the throne of England, to be king in his own right. His wife, Mary, daughter of the deposed King James, had fortunately been raised as an Anglican, and was the heir presumptive to the English throne. So, from then on, they were always referred to as King William and Mary as though it was one word.

Early on in the piece, Louis IV had made a pact with Charles to gang up against William of Orange. Louis didn't understand that Charles's word was not necessarily his bond, and when a better offer came along he took it. Charles married his niece off to William, and Louis, who was by this time very old (he was on the throne 75 years), was furious. Here he was having wars all over the shop, trying to grab land and William of Orange goes and marries Mary of England. He was livid. Between them, William and Mary had the biggest and best navy around. William was rich and he had threatened Louis's possessions in the Low Countries, and now he had England as well. So Louis decided what he needed was a peace treaty. England, plus the Netherlands, were both formidable, and going to war with them didn't seem like such a good idea. The only problem was the English were having trouble finding a diplomat who was able to negotiate a treaty while coping with all the French etiquette. It was a minefield. To whom should one bow? Who had precedence over whom? There was no one in England who could cope with it, until they found Hans Bentinck, Duke of Portland.

He knew exactly how to behave and was quite capable of outdoing the French in their quintessential Frenchness!

William was a good administrator but he made a couple of rather large mistakes. The first was to get a bunch of city traders together and let them issue shares. The result was the Bank of England and the national debt. When he came over from Holland, he brought with him some chums and naturally wanted to give them somewhere nice to live, so he started giving them great chunks of Ireland. This really didn't go down at all well. They were Protestants; Ireland was a Catholic country. Honestly - what was he thinking? The repercussions of what he did are still felt today.

Mary died fairly early in the piece, leaving William to rule alone. William was good at some things, but what he wasn't so good at was being a soldier. He was no strategist but, like a lot of people who think they are good at everything, he wouldn't leave Churchill in charge of the army and wanted to take the lead in every battle, most of which England promptly lost, leaving France and Louis on a high.

CHAPTER 23

Queen Anne and the Spanish War of Succession

After William's death, Queen Anne came to the throne. She was a chubby lady with a chubby husband, Prince George of Denmark. All they wanted was a reasonably quiet Protestant life and to eat good food, but what they got was the Spanish War of Succession.

The last of the Spanish Habsburgs died in 1700. Louis immediately demanded they put his grandson on the throne. The rest of Europe didn't actually see it that way, quite rightly feeling that Louis was making another grab for more power. The Austrian, Bavarian, English and God knows how many other countries thought they had a right to Spain and its colonies. No doubt the Turks felt the same way after the way they'd been treated.

Russia rarely got themselves involved in these battles unless it had to do with sea ports. They were virtually a land-locked country, although they popped out occasionally to see what the rest of the world was doing. They tended to stay away from European politics, until it occurred to Peter the Great that the countries who did well and were the richest were clearly the ones with the largest navies.

China seemed to have little interest in the Western World, apart from selling them things. With a bow and an inscrutable smile, they would complete a deal and then seemingly disappear back behind the bamboo-curtain. Their cache of medical and scientific breakthroughs remaining a treasure-trove of knowledge undiscovered by the West for centuries.

Meanwhile, the Austrians were taking over practically all of Spain's possessions, except for Spain itself.

Queen Anne had a very bossy friend, Sarah Jennings, and for the sake of a peace Anne usually went along with whatever Sarah wanted. What Anne herself wanted, however, was to live a quiet life with her tubby husband and produce an heir to the throne. She had seventeen children (most of whom sadly died at birth), with the oldest surviving until he was about ten. What Sarah wanted was something else entirely. She had fallen madly in love with John Churchill, and he with her, and there was no doubt he was one of the world's great military minds, so what Sarah wanted was for John to steam off to the various battles involved with the Spanish succession. And, despite the queen's reluctance to be involved, this is exactly what he ended up doing, and he did it splendidly.

The only battle I know much about is Blenheim, which the British won because of Churchill's military skills. It was a great victory (mainly because Churchill didn't do what everyone was expecting him to do). Warfare in those days was quite gentlemanly, if you didn't mind killing a lot of people; you fought a bit, then you had a rest (generally about tea time), then you fought a bit more.

Churchill ignored all that; he marched his troops straight along the Danube for two hundred and fifty miles without stopping. It took five weeks. Because they were next to the river, he could float whatever supplies he needed along with him. And when the battle began he also didn't stop. The French were totally confused by such ungentlemanly behaviour, and they were decimated. So the battle of Blenheim was a brilliant success for the British.

Sarah, who by then had married John, bullied Anne into giving John a dukedom and land so he could build himself a palace, and of course the money to so. Eventually, Sarah annoyed Anne one too many times by telling her to be quiet (as Anne was addressing parliament which hardly seemed the brightest thing to do, even if your husband was adored by everyone) and promptly got herself banished from the court.

Anne did end up making Churchill a duke (and he thus became the Duke of Marlborough). Sarah ended up spending most of her time bickering with builders.

While we're here, I have to mention one of the things they did get right in the film "The Favourite" (which actually sort of annoyed me otherwise). It was in showing just how boring life could often be for the upper class. Clearly, if they weren't fighting a war or in government, the upper echelons evidently had to find various ways to amuse themselves (mainly weekends staying at chums country houses, where the main sport was bed-hopping. So that after a male heir was born, no one really knew exactly who the father was). Plus, according to the screenwriters of the film, their supposedly posh pastimes included bizarre hobbies such as goose-racing and strange makeshift sports, such as throwing pomegranates at a naked fat man. I don't know about those, but of course I do know they shot at anything that could run or fly, and then there was the ghastly dog-baiting, and bare-knuckle fighting (virtually to the death – at least, that was until the 19th century when the Marquis of Queensberry popped out of the woodwork and put some rules into boxing).

One truly odd thing about Queen Anne is that in the book, "1066 and All That," they keep referring to her as "'The Dead Queen". She may have been a bit dull but she was alive at some stage. At school if people said something stupid or something that we already knew, we'd say, "Oh, Queen Anne is dead!", meaning it was old news. There must have been some reason for people saying the poor woman was dead when there was a time she patently was not, but at first I couldn't discover what it was. I dug about. (This was a bit like assembling furniture from IKEA. You fiddle about and fiddle about trying to put it together until finally, in desperation and irritation, you actually read the instructions.) I was rabbiting on about it for days until my ex said with equal irritation,

"Why don't you look it up?" (He probably meant "Google it", but I don't like doing that. I prefer books.) I finally looked it up in one of my history books and found that when she really had died, they decided to pretend she was still alive until a fresh (that is, non-Catholic) candidate for the next King or Queen could be found. So, until they did, she ruled "in absentia" (one can hardly be more absent than being dead!), as it were. Everybody knew, but, being British, no one talked about it, except for the occasionally whispered "Queen Anne is dead" (which, strangely, seems to have caught on and was still being said centuries later).

The next nearest to the throne was a Catholic and they couldn't have that. So, there was a hell of a flap with them going back into history, looking at who married whom and constant queries as to whether they were indeed Protestant or not, and whether it would be possible that they could actually take over the English throne?

About this time Louis XIV's wife died. For some time, he had had a mistress, Madam de Maintenon. She had a completely different idea about how Louis should conduct himself (which basically meant there was to be no more frivolous parties or bed-hopping). Religion was the thing and one should do good works. He did build a hospital in Paris (the Hotel des Invalides, rather like the Chelsea Pensioners), to look after soldiers wounded in his various wars. She, meanwhile, built a school to educate young girls. Louis XIV died in 1715, having out-lived practically everybody (but not having finished building his big house). He actually died of gangrene (which, back in the day, must have been a very nasty way to go), and he was succeeded by his great-great-grandson Louis XV (who was all of five years old!).

CHAPTER 24

Peter the Great

I only found out how interesting he was while I was watching a documentary about him. Before we go one step further, let's be clear: the Russians really were barbarians. People tended to try not to get into wars with them as there were always more Russians to be thrown into the battle, and the whole thing was usually bloody and dreadful. The Romanovs came to power by committee! (So much for "divine right"!) When the dynasty before them died out no one was quite sure what to do or whom to put in its place, and so they voted in the Romanovs. As far as I can see the first three were rather dull.

When Aleksei, the first Romanov Tsar, died he left the throne to Peter's half-brother Fedor I. However, Fedor was sickly and only lasted till 1682. His mother, who was Aleksei's second wife, thrust Peter and his elder brother Ivan forward and pronounced they would rule jointly. (Though she must have been aware that her step-son, Ivan, sixteen at the time, was both mentally and physically ill, and would not be doing much ruling.) Peter, who was only ten at the time, couldn't have cared less; all he wanted to do was play with ships. Russia was basically land-locked, but he didn't care; ships were the thing as far as he was concerned. He took himself over to the Netherlands to learn how to build ships. Being slightly suspicious as to why he wanted any ships at all (while reminding themselves that he came from a land-locked country), the Dutch nevertheless gave Peter a ship and basically said, "Here, have a ship, now go away and don't bother us!".

So, then Peter took himself off to England, where he learnt more about ships and how to build them, working alongside the builders. He also went to Greenwich to see the telescope because he was very interested in science. Basically, though, he was completely uncouth under a thin coat of sophistication. He'd never seen a wheelbarrow before and so he and his entourage had wheelbarrow races up and down the street, managing to kill quite a lot of people (which the Russian found hysterically funny, the English not so much). I was talking to a writer friend about this and he said perhaps wheelbarrows had, at the time only just been invented, so I looked them up and apparently the Egyptians had used them when building the pyramids, then China apparently refined them and they made their way along the Silk Road to Europe very early on, bypassing Russia (as most people seemed to do at the time).

(Apropos nothing in particular, China kept itself to itself, as did Russia, but the upper echelon became highly educated, deeply involved in all things new, especially medicine and science. Nevertheless, the Chinese lower class were quite as barbaric as the Russians were. Things looked very beautiful on the outside, but their favourite way of killing people was to take a live person and cut a thousand pieces out of him; not my idea of a civilized nation.)

Russia just plodded along, ignoring everyone unless it wanted a piece of someone else's land. Peter's little trip to the outside world did make the powers that be begin to think maybe there were things out there worth looking at.

Once he knew how to build ships, Peter was ready to go home. When he left the place where he and his henchmen had been staying it was wrecked, with its beautiful furniture smashed to pieces and its gorgeous pictures all ripped up. It must have been something along the lines of how the rock bands used to behave in the 1960s, with tales of TVs being thrown out of hotel windows and people riding their motorbikes up and down the halls of The Chelsea Hotel. Who would have guessed that such errant behaviour had parallels with history's Peter the Great?

Peter announced that he was going home to Russia to build himself a navy. Everyone looked at each other in disbelief, asking, "What does he want a navy for in Russia, it's land-locked?"

"Well," said someone or other, hopefully, "perhaps he'll play at sea-battles like he did with the wheelbarrows!" (without so many people dying, perhaps?). However, they soon all discovered this was not the idea at all.

Once back in Russia, the first thing Peter did was depose his step-sister who had taken over ruling the place and was very bossy. He soon put a stop to that and had her sent to a nunnery. (It's amazing how useful nunneries were through the ages; every time a king or someone in power wanted to get rid of a female relative who they felt was being a nuisance, it was the classic line made immortal by Shakespeare, "Get thee to a nunnery!" It didn't seem to happen with men. I can't remember anyone ever supposedly saying, "Get thee to a monastery!" I think they just tended to get straight to the point instead and chopped off men's heads. Interestingly, in Elizabethan times "nunnery" was also slang for a brothel, so Hamlet may have been telling Ophelia to lose her virtue rather preserve it in an actual nunnery.)

Once he was home and settled, as well as building ships, Peter decided everyone should dress fashionably like the other Europeans, and beards were the first thing to go! Naturally, as a beard was apparently part of the Russian Orthodox religion, a big fuss was created. Peter resolved that if one wanted to keep his beard, he had to pay a sort of levee. If you chose to do this, you were then presented with a small disc which had to worn at all times. They had been far happier dressed in their traditional Russian clothes: heavy boots and thick pants with long, fur-lined coats, which may not have been elegant but they certainly did suit the Russian climate. That said, with his the peculiarly Russian talent for annoying people, there were things much higher on Peter's list of priorities at this stage than what his subjects wore, as he was coming up with a load of other plans.

Ivan, Peter's simple-minded half-brother - and supposed co-ruler - died around this time at the age of twenty-nine.

The world soon discovered what exactly Peter intended to do with his new-found ship-building skills. Obviously, once he started all this ship-building, he needed a port to the outside world. The world watched with interest as to what was he going to do. They confronted the Netherlands, asking, "Why on earth did you give Peter the Great a ship?".

"We only gave him the one ship; what's he going to do with that?" replied the Netherlands.

"Well, he's got 20 of the damned things now," replied the rest of the world and then they all waited to see what Peter would do. His eyes fell on the Baltic Sea which was under the control of Sweden, and he started a very bloody and nasty war, which lasted for several years. A whole bunch of people joined in (it gave me a headache trying to work out who was on whose side). Peter finally won, and got himself a sea port on the Baltic. The Swedes swore, "Well, we're not doing that again!", and world was now aware of Russia as a military power.

Around 1703, Peter began to build a city. It was on very swampy land and in the building of St. Petersburg a hundred-thousand lives were lost.

Peter the Great had also discovered the riches countries in the world were those with large navies, so they were able to trade with the rest of the world. The fact that the rest of the world was beginning to dislike Russia intensely and was quite nervous about it didn't upset him a bit.

Russia was so big and there were so many of its citizens available to be called in to any given fight that Peter had no compunction in throwing more and more peasants into the fray (clearly without any consideration for them, whatsoever). The rest of the world sat back and watched Peter with some trepidation.

CHAPTER 25

More Historical Trivia that Struck Me as Interesting

After the battle for the Spanish Succession, Philippe V, a Bourbon (and the grandson of Louis XIV), became King of Spain. (The Bourbons are still around because I met one. He was the cousin of the present King of Spain, who was going out with a girlfriend of mine.) However, all this fighting to try to enlarge the empire had left France practically broke.

Peter the Great popped into Europe, had a look round and was impressed with what he saw. He frightened young King Louis to death by picking him up and hugging him in a big Russian bear-hug. As no one normally touches the royal personage, the child was really scared, but got over his fright when the huge man put him down and smiled at him. When he left France, as I said, Peter started to build St. Petersburg.

Back in Britain the English and the Scots were bickering again about who was king of what and the English Parliament brought in something called "The Alien Act".

I don't really think they thought the Scots were little green men from another planet. In fact, I don't think such beings had been thought of at that stage, but it was still called "The Alien Act", although it didn't last all that long.

Because there appeared little chance of Anne having a child who would live long enough to become king or queen, and because most of the people who actually could lay claim to the throne were Catholic, the government (under Walpole) produced the Act of Succession. This basically meant that the monarch had to be a member of the Church of England.

The fuss about who could or couldn't be king or queen after Anne became quite frantic as they struggled to find someone to fit the bill. Her half-brother Charles was the nearest heir, but he was Catholic, so they went digging around until they came up with George of Hanover, who was a second cousin, once removed - to God knows who - but Protestant! So he was really the only game in town.

As I mentioned earlier, up until this time most kings, emperors and the like were convinced they were placed in their regal positions by "divine right". Although King John had got a nasty fright with the Magna Carta, and of course Charles I got his head chopped off because he kept telling everyone he was king and had a "divine right" to do what he liked. I think if you'd done a survey about that time, they'd have still said, "Yes, I'm here by divine right". However, exactly why they considered that to be so is completely beyond me, especially in view of all the fighting some of them did in order to get where they were in the first place! One wonders how much ale they'd been drinking and if they were actually quite sane!

CHAPTER 26

The Georges

And so…we're into the Georges. Let's be abundantly clear about this one too: The Hanovers were really quite weird. Despite that - or maybe because of that - they were sort of suited to ruling Hanover, but not so much suited to the taking over as a world power. Though a German Royal House, they at various times ruled not only Hanover, but also Great Britain and Ireland. In a lot of ways they were just plain, if not actually mad, odd. To start with, not one of the fathers could stand their first-born sons and often refused to talk to them at all. And they had a distinct dislike of letting their daughters marry anyone if they could help it. The first two didn't speak English, and although England was a far greater power, they liked life in cozy Hanover (where there was no doubt how "divine" they were). They all loved music and most of them played some sort of instrument. And, as you may know, they also adopted Handel as a substitute English composer.

In 1682, George I married his first cousin (as was the royal way of the era, unwittingly throwing caution to the wind as far as in-breeding!). George married Sophia of Celle and they had two children. As George was actually having an affair on the side (also, as you know, a very royal tradition), Sophia thought she was entitled to have an affair too. She fell in love with a Swedish count. But, apparently, kings can have affairs but queens can't, and so the poor count was hacked to death; the marriage between George and Sophia was dissolved and she was locked up for the rest of her life, not to see her children again for thirty years. Not only odd, but not very nice either! There was a very sad film made about it.

George's coronation couldn't be called a success; everyone booed. England was not at all sure it wanted a fat German king who couldn't (or wouldn't) learn to speak English and preferred Hanover anyway. The fact that he could prefer a small backward state somewhere in Germany to England really got up the nose of the average Englishman (who didn't want him there in the first place), particularly when he made it perfectly clear he thought he was doing them a great favour coming over to be king. He also left his eldest son and heir to be brought up in Hanover; not a very sensible idea for someone who would presumably be taking over the role of king of England! His subjects were discontented but soldiered on. But what's life without a war? And so, the Jacobite rebellion broke out.

The Scots were led by John Erskine, the 23rd (or 6th, counting from 1565 when a recount began) Earl of Mar, the chief Scottish Jacobite, aided and abetted by the French. (For some reason I don't understand, the Duke of Marlborough seemed to be on the side of the Scots.) Anyway, it didn't last all that long and the Jacobite's lost. This left the Catholics crushed and many a Catholic house built in England in that period had a "priests' hole". This was a place where, if for some reason they had a visiting priest, he would hide if the local militia descended on the house searching for Roman Catholic priests.

With all this fighting going on, the government couldn't pay the navy, so the Bank of England came up with the brilliant idea of having a lottery. It seemed like a good idea at the time and was alright to begin with but it ended up making the national debt even bigger. Then we had the South Sea Bubble - another grand scheme to make money. The British South Sea Trading company had been around for a while but it wanted to try to get into the South American market. In 1719 it offered to take over the national debt by selling shares in the company. What was considered a good idea turned into a disaster. The company enticed the stockholders to convert their high interest stocks into low interest tradable bonds. Buying and selling shares became a frenzy. People crippled themselves to get their hands-on shares and the price went up and up until the bubble burst. It was just like the 1929 crash. Don't people ever learn anything from history?

At first, George tried to take an interest in the politics of the land, hampered slightly by the fact he couldn't speak a word of English and had no idea what people were talking about, and was still clinging to being divinely right. This didn't work too well. Because of George's deficiency, the government had, by that stage, got a strong hold on the way things were done. Sir Robert Walpole was in charge and became the first Prime Minister of Great Britain.

When George's son arrived from Hanover with his wife and children, the king immediately had a fight with him and took the kids away from their parents. George apparently quite liked little children; what he couldn't stand was adults with ideas of their own. Walpole tried to patch things up between father and son, but it didn't work. Finally, George left Walpole to run the country and took himself back to Hanover (where he had a "divine right"), so he could annoy anyone he pleased.

One odd piece of information I found interesting is that when George arrived in London he was amazed to find it much cleaner than most of the cities in Europe, and the people healthier. It was newer, in parts, and cleaner, because the Great Fire had burnt most of it down and they'd had to rebuild, and they were healthier because of the fashion for drinking tea which entailed having to boil the water.

Not having been a great success as a king, George I died in 1727, leaving the throne to his much-disliked son George II. He settled in but wanted to be more involved with the political side of things, which Walpole wasn't about to allow. Another annoying German wanting to steer what was - at the time - a reasonably steady ship.

George, however, was a good soldier. Somewhere around this time Rob Roy went to war with England and took Scotland back from them. (I had always thought Rob Roy was a figment of Walter Scott's imagination.)

Then George's wife, whom he loved dearly, died. As she was dying, she begged him to re-marry. "Oh, no my love," he said, "I'll just have mistresses."

He was the last king of England to actually go into battle and apparently was very brave in leading his men into the fray.

CHAPTER 27

The War of Jenkins' Ear and Other Peculiarities

Did you know you could go to war over an ear? Imagine how bored you'd have been to start something like that? Throwing pomegranates at fat people is stupid enough but to start an entire war over an ear? When an English merchant ship was boarded by Spanish coastguards the attackers cut off Captain Robert Jenkins' ear. As piracy had been around forever most people took this as a part of life at sea, but the British South Sea Company decided that a victorious war with Spain would boost its trade in the Caribbean. And the wrong done to this man should be righted. When you hear things like that you must think television is not so bad. What started as a small skirmish turned into the War of the Austrian Succession, much to the delight of the Prince of Wales, who was allowed to take part in this very military-sounding affair. Interestingly, the British used a regiment of American troops.

The war developed because some Austrian territory was ruled by Salic Law, which said women couldn't inherit, and when Charles VI died only Maria Theresa remained and she was not allowed to reign without a male consort. Maria Theresa had loads of daughters also called Maria (Marie Antoinette being one of them). They kept popping up married to one or other of the Catholic kings or princes who were around at the time. (I'll say more on Maria Theresa later.)

A book I read about Austria, Russia and the various German principalities firmly stated that most of their monarchs or Emperors were barking mad, presumably because of all the inter-marrying of cousins (usually Bavarians!). There were a few sane ones, but the crazies are the fascinating ones!

No matter what was suggested, Silesia didn't want to belong to Austria. The simplest solution was to hand it over to a country that had kings. But why do that when the War of Jenkins' Ear was going so nicely and slides quite easily into the War of the Austrian Succession? It kept people busy for about eight years because Silesia would keep on about not having a woman on the throne.

Soon everyone was involved with the Austrian succession. As well as France, England and the Dutch, who really had nothing to do with it but then decided to get involved anyway, there were Prussia and the Electorate of Bavaria while on the Austrian side were Hungary, Croatia, the Netherlands, Bohemia and Italy, and I suppose somewhere the Turks were there too.

When it ended all that had been achieved apart from the money it cost and the people it killed was precisely nothing, except Silesia left the Austrian umbrella, which is what it should have done in the first place, and Fredrick the Great of Prussia gained Silesia. I don't know what they were all getting so excited about; it wasn't a sea port, which is what they mainly seemed to fight over. I suppose it had given them something to do for eight years. Football hadn't been invented, and cricket didn't seem to take on at the time anywhere but England, so there was a large gap to be filled.

No one really took much notice of America at this stage although it was involved in the War of Austrian Succession, fighting on the English side. As far as most people were concerned, America was a place that produced cotton and tobacco and various other things and was somewhere to dump unwanted criminals.

In England, Parliament had two parties, namely, the Whigs and the Tories.

The Whigs were mainly from the aristocracy and the Tories didn't seem to have been very much different. The Whigs believed in constitutional government, which had them in conflict for much of the time with the monarchy. However, with the early Georges not speaking English, the government gained a far greater grip on events.

As I've said, all the Georges really disliked their eldest sons. It must have been an inherited trait. Prince Fredrick, who could not only speak English but who also took an active interest in politics, played cricket and did all sorts of English-type-things, also spent money like water. His father really didn't like him! He refused to give him any money, so Frederick borrowed from rich friends. Whatever he did the people liked him. He was very charming and not a stultifying bore like his father. Fredrick's interest in politics used to get up his father's nose, especially as Fredrick thought the monarchy should be constitutional and not rule by some mad "divine right", but that was the concept his father was used to ruling by as that's what they did in Hanover.

How did one get to be king or queen? Did they fight until the other side gave up? Were you born to it? Or were you somebody's cousin and when a vacancy popped up, someone said, "You'll make a good king; in you go."? And was it the office that made you "divine" over time? Or were you "divine" from the start of when you became king or queen? Most confusing.

For some reason (probably because he didn't get along with his father at all), when Fredrick visited his parents with his heavily pregnant wife, as she went into labour he whisked her away, dragging her, plus three children and sundry other people, off to his own house. His father went ballistic (and I don't think his poor wife could have been very keen on the idea either) as, apparently, the king was supposed to be present at the birth of any royal child. Unfortunately, the child was stillborn.

When the Prince of Wales got himself shot (but not fatally) on a visit to Drury Lane, George couldn't contain himself. "Why are they shooting at him? He's not king; I am!", he complained.

Then suddenly everyone was drinking gin. To try to stop half the nation being more drunk than usual (and as too much gin tended to kill people), parliament passed The Gin Act, which taxed the sellers and put the price up enormously.

The Prince of Wales told them it wouldn't work, and of course it didn't. Apart from making most of the country furious, too much of the populace started distilling their own gin and some of the things they put in it killed people sooner than it would have if they were drinking commercial gin, so that act got repealed fairly quickly.

Then the Methodists jumped in. They flocked into London, going to the poorer parts where the drinking-plague was rife and they ranted and raved at the drinkers that God was very much annoyed with them and that they had to immediately stop drinking. These were the days when God was always at the feast, everyone went to church and everyone adhered to some sort of religion, so to have Him personally cross with them was a catastrophe! Life was hard enough without the omnipresent personage looking down breathing fire and brimstone. So what the government failed to accomplish, the Methodists seemed to have instead achieved to a large degree.

The school I went to, dear reader, was in a house that either belonged to John Wesley, leader of the Methodists, or was where he spent a lot of time. Our dormitory was built with a sort of platform that he used to preach from. Being thirteen-year-old girls, we preached from it too, though I don't think some of the things we said would have gone down at all well with the Methodists. Looking at pictures of the early Methodists, they were a rather grim and quite chubby lot, who look though they are in the middle of a bout of very bad indigestion. They tended to go off to places in Africa as missionaries, where they basically bullied the poor people they found over there into believing in Christianity.. Some of the Africans, however, didn't want to know about it, and discovered that missionaries made a rather good lunch..

Most people thought Fredrick, the prince of Wales, would make an excellent king but, unfortunately, he died in 1751, leaving his son George (who was not in the least prepared to be king) to take on the role. He had the advantage (for the first time in Georgian history) that his father didn't hate him. So, after George II's death in 1760, Prince Frederick's eldest son became George III. He was a sweet man, but seemingly mad for much of the time (there is argument today as to whether this was caused by a physical illness called porphyria, or was, as it appeared to be, a mental-health problem). In his saner moments he was a family man who loved his wife and children and would spend hours playing with them. He didn't have mistresses and he liked small children, but like the two Georges before him he wasn't so keen on them when they grew up. And he had no intention of letting any of his daughters get married if he could help it. He didn't have much interest in politics; what he really wanted was to be was a farmer.

CHAPTER 28

Rebellions and Other Goings-On

Meanwhile, back in France, Charles Stuart was thinking it might be a good idea to have another go at getting England back. The French sent an emissary to check out the feeling among the Jacobites. It was thought a very good move at the time and everyone was quite keen on the idea. Thinking it might be a good idea, however, and actually doing something, was very different.

The French gave Charles two ships that were immediately lost in a storm, which should have given him some idea about how things were going to go. Although he had only the Scottish and English Jacobites to help him, he did rather well to begin with and got nearly to Derby. Then George II sent his son, the Duke of Cumberland, after him and he chased him back into the Highlands, where it all came to a terrible end in the Battle of Culloden. (I've been there and you can still feel the sadness where so many very brave Highlanders died.) Charlie escaped with the help of Flora MacDonald who dressed him up as her maid and rowed him over to the island of Skye. If nothing else this is another one of those situations that also happened to inspire a very nice song.

Cumberland then took the whole thing much too far. He basically devastated the entire Highlands until nothing was left standing and those who escaped the slaughter fled (mainly to Canada) and that's how you can tell the Canadian accent from the American. Those Canadians who aren't speaking French have a slight burr and say "hoose" instead of "house". (It's quite odd, come to think of it, that whenever something bad happens to the Irish they seem to go to America, but when something happens to the Scots they go to Canada.)

When Cumberland returned to London, he was hailed as a great hero, but as word trickled down about what had really happened, everyone turned against him in horror. One might not care for the Jacobites, nor the Scots for that matter, but it wasn't "British" to go slaughtering everyone in such an uncivilized fashion. Mind you, it was obviously very Hanoverian, (i.e., nothing to do with England at all).

CHAPTER 29

More Trivia

The year 1756 began with the Seven Years War with everyone in Europe involved, for some reason. Most saw it as a grab by France to acquire more land and it sort of grew out the War of the Austrian Succession, which had really achieved nothing. Silesia attached itself to Russia, which it should have done in the first place. So, it was, "Let the battle commence! Round two!"

Silesia, having become part of the Russian empire, soon realised this wasn't going to work, as, not long after, Russia itself had an empress.

The British East India Company had been in existence for years but, as it grew larger, it always seemed to be at war with someone or other. Supposedly, Clive of India managed to get over a hundred people in a Black Hole of Calcutta for some strange reason and when they opened it up the next day, only twenty-three were still alive. But what they were doing there in the first place, I have no idea.

Despite all the fighting with people with extraordinary names, the East India Company became very powerful dealing in silk, salt, indigo, tea and opium. This led to a clash with the Dutch East India Company.

A year after Europe had declared peace on itself everyone sat around twiddling their thumbs until someone said, ' "Well this is very boring, let's have a war," and so they did. Then George II died, leaving George III in charge.

CHAPTER 30

Louis XV

Louis XV obviously came after Louis XIV, only he was his great-grandson. He came to the throne when he was five, after his eldest brother had died of smallpox and both he and the next in line got measles. The doctors bled his elder brother, but Louis had a very bossy nanny who told the doctors to leave him alone so while his older brother died, Louis recovered and actually finished building Versailles. Until he came of age, Phillip II Duke of Orleans and Cardinal Fleury governed in his stead.

As I mentioned earlier, Peter the Great made another visit and being Russian gave the young man a huge bear-hug, swung him round and kissed him, probably scaring the young man nearly to death, but when Louis discovered he wasn't about to be killed they became good friends, both being interested in science and various other things.

Louis' reign for the first few years was managed by Cardinal Fleury who had some sort of a fight with the deposed king of Poland and got France mixed up in the Seven Years War.

Louis the XV was a sort of non-event king as far as I can see, but he did have two interesting mistresses. One, Madame de Pompadour, ended up as his friend and adviser and was the only one who would tell him the truth.

In Austria, Maria Theresa was allowed to reign only if she had a male consort. She was fascinating, deeply Catholic, loathed the Jews and Protestants, wasn't all that keen on the Greek Orthodox, and wasn't too sure how she felt about the Jesuits, although I think a lot of people felt the same way. I doubt she actually came across any Muslims as they belonged to the Ottoman Empire, which was to be attacked whenever necessary. Maria Theresa loved children, which was just as well as she gave birth to sixteen, though only ten survived. She lost three daughters before one actually lived, named Maria Carolina.. (I've visited the Hofburg Palace in Vienna. It's big and rambling but is actually like a home. You can imagine living there, whereas most palaces you'd have to be insane to want to spend any time there.)

Maria Theresa was so anti the Jews and the Protestants- although she did not got to the extent that the Spanish did - that she wanted to ban them from Austria,. Her son Joseph, who was by this time co-ruler, managed to persuade her this was not a good idea. When he pointed out that one of her chief advisors was Jewish, and was practically running the country, she backed down.

Sometimes one wonders if she was unhinged, like so much royalty over the years. Incredibly religious, she spent most of her pregnancy before Joseph was born on her knees, praying for a son. When he did arrive, she kept referring to him as "Saint Joseph." Very hard on a little boy, I would think, although he seems to have turned out all right, if a bit autocratic.

When her daughter-in-law, Josepha of Bavaria, went down with smallpox, Maria Theresa insisted on nursing her and naturally caught smallpox herself. Poor Josepha died and Maria Theresa pulled through, but dragged her daughter, Josepha - you'd really think with all the names available they could come up with some others - to pray with her over Josepha's open coffin. It apparently didn't occur to her magnificent self that there was a very large likelihood that her poor daughter might catch the disease and die; which of course she did. There was much rending of robes and gnashing of teeth and Maria never really got over it. She planned to marry as many of her children off to the various Catholic kingdoms around the place so she could stick her nose into their foreign policies via her children and make a bloody nuisance of herself.

Did you know you could have a war about a dog? The war of the Pomeranian was in the middle of the Austrian War of Succession. I've never heard of a place called Pomerania. However, given the way minds worked in those days, it is perfectly possible that an innocent Pomeranian was sitting somewhere, probably Poland, doing no harm to anyone when suddenly everyone decided started to pick on it, so it was attacked and they called it the War of the Pomeranian. As far I'm concerned it was a war over a dog. I can think of far better dogs to go to war about, Labradors, Saint Bernard's, Huskies, Red Setters are nice although daft, perhaps Standard Poodles, even Pugs are cute. If I were war-like, I could go to war over a Pug, I think. Though apparently their breath smells. Who actually won the Pomeranian and what they wanted it for in the first place remains a mystery? Usually when something is won there's a statue somewhere.... Nothing, not even best dog in show. Mind you there isn't anything to show who won Jenkins Ear, which I suppose is reasonable; who on earth would want to look at a bloody ear?

Whatever happened, the country is no longer around but the dogs are. So perhaps if you can go to war over an ear, why not a dog? Perhaps there was a war concerning small furry beasts. Who knows?

Maria Theresa loved music and there is a big painting in the Hofburg Palace of a huge gathering of people and in the right-hand corner is a small boy, Mozart. Maria Theresa used to sit him on her knee and feed him sweets.

The seventeenth and eighteenth centuries were positively littered with interesting women: Nell Gwynn, Lady Georgiana Devonshire and her sister Henrietta (who was Princess Diana's - heaven knows how many greats - aunt), the Bessboroughs, the Ponsonbys, and the Lamb family, who gave us Lord Melbourne eventually, though that was a little later on. Before that he was William Lamb and married Caroline Bessborough, who then became Caroline Lamb, and she definitely deserves a mention. It was these three families who basically ran London society and its politics. They were Whigs, the most famous of them being the Prime Ministers, the two Pitts, elder and younger (we're nothing if not original, the English), and of course, Lord Melbourne.

Lady Mary Montague, Jane Austen and, later on, all those Brontes are the ones that interest me, some because they were involved in other things that I'll go into later.

Mary Worsley Montague had been stationed with her husband in Istanbul and the Turks - who were far more advanced in medicine than the West - fascinated her. She discovered that a person inoculated with a very small amount of smallpox virus appeared to stay safe from the disease. When she returned to England, she tried to interest the medical profession in her ideas. They thought she was mad. So she suggested a deal they give her six inmates of Newgate Prison who were about to be hanged. She would inject them and if they recovered, they would be allowed to go free. A deal was stuck. She injected the six and they all got better. If they went free or not, I'm not sure.

CHAPTER 31

Catherine the Great

Catherine was German and came from one of those little principalities Germany once bristled with. It's all too confusing, but it was finally worked out that Catherine should marry Peter, the son of Elizabeth, the Empress of Russia. Fortunately, she got on extremely well with her mother-in-law, far better than she did with her own mother, who tended to be very bossy and had an inclination to meddle. Which one should never do; one doesn't walk into a foreign country and imagine you know how to run it better - except of course if you're Napoleon

Catherine was quite startled at first by the Russian habit of everyone throwing their arms round her and kissing her, which was very different from the rather stand-offish German way of behaving but she was determined to fit in. She threw herself into learning Russian and was equally passionate about joining the Russian Orthodox Church.

She was merely sixteen when married to Peter, who was seventeen and still playing with toy soldiers (of course, being him, he may have been planning military strategies rather than simply playing). He took an intense dislike to his bride. They lived apart most of the time but she did have two children. One died very early, and as for the other one, no one knew who his actual father was. Catherine had discovered sex! Throughout her life she had many lovers, but they all seemed to be useful to her. Whether it was ever love or only the next step up the ladder, who knows? But she was the right person for the right time, which seems to have been quite rare, and she doesn't appear to have been roaring drunk half the time as so many others were.

When the Empress Elizabeth died, Catherine found herself in a terrible position. She was stuck with an incredibly childish, if not mad, husband who liked to play with soldiers, and although they had recently come out of the Seven Years War in which Russia had done rather well, Peter wanted to go on fighting people and now had a real army to play with. He dragged Russia into all kinds of strife until it became obvious that he had to go. Catherine, backed by the army, forced him to sign his resignation. Now there was no dispute about her right to the throne, but no-one chopped off his head or sent him to a monastery - as long as he went a long way away!

The stories about the identity of her remaining son's father were hushed up. She was certainly very fond of sex, and one tale suggested she may have had sex with a horse. To say nothing of this being very weird, it must have been bloody uncomfortable for all concerned, and is probably untrue.

She then turned her attention to sea ports. It was nice having a port on the Baltic Sea but it took ages to get from there to the Mediterranean Sea, so she decided to take on the Ottoman Empire. People were beginning to be frightened of Russia's military power, there were such a lot of them, and Catherine didn't seem to care how many of them got killed as long as she eventually got what she wanted. She defeated the Turks and made Russia dominant in the Black Sea.

She also dragged Russia into the industrial age, with iron factories, china factories and all sorts of things. She loved the Arts, built the Hermitage, and collected vast amounts of paintings. As well as all that, she kept up a correspondence with Voltaire until he died, and, in all, she really was quite an all-round interesting lady.

CHAPTER 32

The Industrial Revolution

The Industrial Revolution turned England upside down and try as I might I can't find anything particularly funny about it. Mention steam engines and I think of trains, but the first steam engine, invented by James Watt, was a just whole lot of pipes filled with steam. However, they did clever things, like driving machines, and therefore were called steam engines. (But it was only when Stephenson came along with his so-called "Rocket" that I considered an actual steam engine train arrived on the scene.)

Thus began the Industrial Revolution which turned pretty little villages into large dirty towns. There had always been weavers but they had worked from home. With the arrival of the huge new machines, the weavers were dragged into the cities and their employers thought they would like to live in ugly houses, one on top of another with virtually no sanitation the employees were usually women and children, working incredibly long hours for low wages. England and the mill owners did extremely well out of the whole thing, producing a new middle-class with money - in fact, often more money than the aristocrats, who'd been happily looking down on them for years. Children as young as five had to crawl around in the dark of the mines, climb inside sooty chimneys, or work beneath the spinning jenny, which replaced the crofters who had always worked at home. It didn't appear to occur to anyone for quite a while that this may not be good for a five-year-old.

The spinning jenny was invented by James Hargreaves in a place called Oswaldtwistle in Lancashire. Oswaldtwistle sounds like one of those German towns we kept getting our royal family from, or somewhere in Wales. This invention sent more people to more factories.

Richard Arkwright invented the water wheel, which was used for carding wool into strands. I don't know what carding wool is, but it sounds relatively harmless, till you get to the bit that it has to be peed on (but in checking I see that was back in Roman times).

The exception to the rule were the Huguenots, whom King Louis XIV had kicked out of France. When Louis had one of his purges against the Huguenots, who were mainly spinners and weavers, tended to flee to Spitalfields in London, where they became famous for never using machines and always spinning and weaving by hand. They tended to always to spin and weave in silk, and became as successful as their brother weavers, who were mainly in the North of England.

Meanwhile the children of England were having a very hard time, what with going down mines, climbing up chimneys and under weaving machines. In their usual fashion the government thought about it, talked about it, but didn't do anything about it.

CHAPTER 33

The Americans

By the early 1770s the Americans were becoming tired of being ignored and used as a sort of dumping ground for stray miscreants that English didn't need. England really didn't take America very seriously at the time. The place was sparsely dotted with immigrants and Native Americans, but with the advent of the railways people started moving around and America started to become a force to be reckoned with, and began making it plain they were getting heartily sick of Britain.

The British parliament took no notice, of course. They saw them as a colony full of rough necks and pilgrims, who had no idea how to run a country (though some of them did appear to be making money). They were taxed very heavily, so the Americans banded together as "The Sons of the Revolution" and announced "No Tax Without Representation". The British ignored this, as they tended to do with people whom they considered a lower class than themselves. "Who do they think they are talking to?" If one looked down one's nose and said "Shoo!", they generally went away. Not the Americans though; when the next load of tea arrived in Boston Harbour, The Sons of the Revolution tipped it into the sea (an event usually referred to as the Boston Tea Party). The East India Company, whose ship it was, and the British were flabbergasted: "They've done what? Have they any idea how expensive tea is?".

The truth was America had had enough and decided to shake off the British yoke. Thirteen states got together to form an army. The first battle was at Bunker Hill, which the British won, but half their soldiers were killed.

I am not going to recite what happened next, mainly because I haven't studied American history and what I do know has probably been gleaned from watching movies. And I have no faith in the screenwriters not having added their own slant on events. Anyway, there were numerous battles involving people like John Hancock and Benedict Arnold. (He's considered to have been very bad, but I'm not sure why, I think he changed sides.)

One of the strangest battles was at Lexington. Everyone was ready. Some shots were fired. They all waited for something more to happen and when it didn't, they all went home.

Now, the rest of the world began to take an interest in America. The Spanish, French and Dutch were all on the side of the revolutionaries, no doubt hoping to regain some of the territories the British had pinched from them in earlier wars. Some North American Indians and some slaves fought on the side of the British.

Paul Revere rode about the country before the Battle of Lexington, yelling "The British are coming!" and frightening everyone to death. This seems slightly pointless as the British were already there!

George Washington was in charge of the Continental Army and fighting battles all over the place, but the deciding one was when he crossed the Delaware River. This was not only the coup de grace, but it occurred in winter and we know how the English feel about that. This came after a whole bunch of treaties had been signed, which no one was particularly interested in honouring. ot one of the countries who came to the aid of the Americans came away with anything, Spain lost Florida to Mexico, and Texas already belonged to Mexico, and the Americans bought Louisiana from the French, which was a deal naturally enough called "The Louisiana Purchase"(Cole Porter wrote a musical about it).

Having won, the Americans declared themselves to be "The United States of America, and George Washington became their first president. Thomas Jefferson wrote the Declaration of Independence, which always reads to me more like, "Wouldn't it be nice if life were really like this?". It said: "We hold this to be true, that all men are created equal…" (yes, except if you were black, Native American, or, of course, women). The Founding Fathers also formed a federal government and set out the laws of the land in the Constitution, which, among other things, gave U.S. citizens the right to bear arms so that a militia could be summoned if needed. (It never seemed to occur to any sensible person at the time it also meant that a couple of hundred years later guns would be on hand to be used by crazy people, or people high on God knows what, and even sometimes children, who could blithely walk into schools and murder their fellow students, or anyone else that was around.) The Klu Klux Klan draped themselves in what appeared to be white sheets and strange pointed top hats and burnt a cross in people's (mainly black people's) front gardens. Is that really the American idea of everyone being equal?

Of course, when Thomas Jefferson wrote the Declaration of Independence, he failed to mention that he himself had slaves, and did so the whole of his adult life. As did four other presidents. As for the later well-meaning phrase "Give us your tired, your poor, your huddled masses…" well, that came back to bite them! But America was a new country, really having no ties to Europe and it had its own way of doing things, and the world went back to sort of ignoring it. Basically, the American Revolution was a success.

Actually, when I was young my main interest in America was in cowboys and Indians. I knew all about Billy the Kid, Davy Crockett, who wore a raccoon skin hat and was also a member of congress, Jessie James and his gang, Doc Holiday and Jim Bowie of knife fame.

We listened to a radio program about "The Wild West ". The Alamo also intrigued me. That was where Mexicans battled Texans and everyone in the Alamo was killed, including Davy Crockett and Jim Bowie. The end result appeared to be Texas joining the Sons of the

Revolution. Then there was the gunfight at the OK Corral. All of these made marvellous films and were part of the American tapestry. I'm not sure if Butch Cassidy and the Sundance kid were real or a figment of William Goldman's imagination, but the film was great. I love good cowboy films.

CHAPTER 34

Australia

Now that the British had nowhere to send their unwanted convicts, Captain James Cook was sent off on an expedition to explore what was became known as 'Terra Australis'. A couple of years earlier, Abel Tasman had put paid to the idea that Australia was some sort of myth, so Cook took Joseph Banks with him to gather information about this new land's flora and fauna. He arrived in what is now known as Botany Bay in 1770, and the British were delighted to find it was in fact there. They had a new place to dispose of their unwanted felons (who had done such "dire" things as, say, stealing a loaf of bread). Interestingly enough, less than five percent of Australia's population is descended from convicts; most were what were known as 'free-settlers', who arrived for various reasons (such as searching for gold or escaping the Irish Potato Famine). In all, it was clear that Terra Australis had clearly become the place to be for one or another reason.

This next fact has little to do with anything really, but my great-great-grandfather was wandering around Southwark street, shopping at eleven o'clock at night - God knows why - when he was set-upon by a thief who stole his watch. It was considered Highway Robbery (I'd always thought Highway Robbery at least consisted of a masked man on a horse on a highway, but apparently not.) The thief – a very unfortunate bloke, really - was caught and hanged. All I can say is that it had better have been a bloody good watch! The whole affair is written up in the records of the Old Bailey, bearing testimony to the fact that the "good old days," were clearly much harsher than one may have imagined!) Oddly enough my ancestor was far more upset about his hat being battered about than the loss of his watch.

Anyway, the First Fleet left England with eleven ships under the guidance of Captain Arthur Phillip in 1787 and arrived in Botany Bay on 26 January 1788. They proceeded to kill off most of the Aboriginal population, not only with weapons

Anyway, the First Fleet left England with eleven ships under the guidance of captain Arthur Phillip in 1787. Arriving in Botany Bay on January 26th 1788. Over time, the new arrivals proceeded to kill off most of the Aboriginal population (they wiped out the whole of Tasmania's Aboriginal population). They also brought with them measles, smallpox, and other diseases that the indigenous people had never encountered before, and with often fatal consequences.

It took a while, but eventually free English settlers began to arrive. Arthur Phillip was made Governor and Sydney started to become a thriving town. Most of the more dangerous and truly difficult convicts were sent to Port Arthur in Tasmania, where they were treated very harshly.

Meanwhile, South Australia forbade any convicts from setting foot on their soil, and put a strictly free-settlers-only policy in place (and the free-settlers-only built churches to put off any convicts).

Another governor of note was Captain Bligh (one of those people who could start a fight in an empty room) of the "Mutiny of the Bounty" fame. He was an excellent seaman, but was a difficult person to deal with and had a violent temper. I don't know exactly what caused the mutiny on the Bounty, but Bligh was put adrift with the sailors who were loyal to him, and it was only his exceptional seamanship that managed to get them to Tahiti in one piece.

Trouble with Captain Bligh started even before this - earlier on, when he was captaining another fleet of ships, he demanded that one of the captains, Joseph Short, be court martialled. The man was sent back to England only to be acquitted. So who in the admiralty thought it would be a good idea for Bligh to become the governor of New South Wales? He was probably making a great nuisance of himself in England, so somebody came up with the idea: "Let's send him to Australia. It's miles away. Perhaps the local wild life will eat him." Considering his seamanship, Cook, who had sailed with him previously, put in a good word, but being captain of a ship is far different from running a colony.

Bligh rubbed everyone up the wrong way, including John MacArthur, who had arrived as an army officer with the second fleet and had stayed on to become a wealthy landowner, introducing Merino sheep to Australia. MacArthur had a lucrative side-line in selling illegal rum to soldiers of the New South Wales Regimental Corps. Being a hot-head, Bligh went in boots first and proceeded to attack MacArthur, not considering for a moment that MacArthur was popular because of the rum, and happened to have the army behind him. There was a riot and Bligh had to hide under the maid's bed. That, and several other things, made the Admiralty decide that perhaps William Bligh was not the man to govern anything, and he was called back to England, hopefully into retirement somewhere a long, long way from other people.

About the same time, Captain Cook had got himself killed in Hawaii.

CHAPTER 35

The Habsburgs Again

Over the years the two Habsburg houses had been trundling along keeping the middle of Europe as safe as possible from the Ottoman Empire and often each other. Some of the emperors were more interesting than others. As mentioned, Maria Theresa was only allowed to reign with a male counterpart, although she was the one who had all the power. She married Francis Stephen of Lorraine and loved him deeply, but got very cross with him because he kept having affairs. Wars went on and on when all they had to do was give up Silesia, which I suppose was important to them, but I can't for the life of me see why.

And there was always Hungary. Whatever Austria wanted it to do, Hungary didn't. It was a bit the same with Poland, though they were a bit quieter about it. Poor Poland; other countries kept dividing it up or plonking their favourite relative in as king, to suit themselves.

On the whole, Maria Theresa was tolerant and a reformer, except where religion was concerned. She disliked the Jews and Protestants and taxed them very heavily. She founded the Vienna General Hospital, and finally made a decision to have all her children inoculated against smallpox after several of her family had died from the disease (with terrific results: no more of them died of smallpox, and the rest of the country followed suit, having their children inoculated too).

She waved a regal paw, passing a bill that required all children to go to school from the age of six to twelve. Great idea, only she didn't look into it - no money, so that didn't happen, unfortunately. It's all very well saying everyone should be educated but you need money to do it. There were still children in the twentieth century in Austria who could not read or write.

Maria Theresa didn't care for the arts, and when her son, the Archduke Ferdinand, suggested that Mozart (whom she had quite liked as a small child) should be given a position at court at the age of 15, she told him not to waste his time with "useless people". Her beloved husband died in 1765 and she went into deep mourning for the rest of her life. She painted all her rooms black, which must have been extremely hard on everyone else.

As a women Maria Theresa could not reign without a male at her side, she reluctantly allowed Joseph, her eldest son (who she had formally called "Saint Joseph,") to reign in name only. She wouldn't let him do anything and they fought all the time. In her mind he became "Joseph the Bloody Nuisance". She was against the partitioning of Poland until she realised that Prussia and Russia were going to do it, with or without her, so she went along with them. However, she came out of the whole thing with Galicia (which has nothing to do with Poland as far as I can see, but she was pleased to have it anyway).

Joseph's first wife, whom he loved dearly, was Isabella of Parma. They had a daughter, named Maria Theresa after her grandmother. Isabella died and Joseph was pushed into marrying Maria Josephine of Bavaria, whom he couldn't stand and whom he refused to be seen with or speak to. Why people who were considered reasonably sane allowed themselves to be pushed into marrying someone they couldn't stand is beyond me. The whole idea of royal marriages was to produce an heir, so it seemed that it was possible to simply marry someone and then basically, never speak to them again. Doesn't seem to be a plan to me. Perhaps she had an enormous dowry.

The Austrian court was nearly as formal as the French and the poor girl was very timid and I think she died of sheer fright after a couple of years into the marriage (although she did have smallpox which may have had something to do with it. Why wasn't she vaccinated?).

Because he didn't get on with his mother, Joseph started to travel. He also tried to get Silesia back. For a little place, it caused an awful lot of trouble. Fredrick the Great of Prussia, who had Silesia at the time, had a fight with Joseph and it cost Joseph the trust of all the other German princes. And still no Silesia. I really don't know what he wanted it for as he owned quite enough of Europe already, and it was hard enough keeping the Hungarians quiet. And of course it was difficult to always keep checking to see who had Poland at any given time.

In 1780 Maria Theresa died, thus getting rid of at least one Maria. (I'm sure if you shouted out "Maria!" in the Viennese court, half the women would stand up; the other half would be Josephinas). Finally, Joseph came into his own. The first thing he did was to take on the churches and really annoy the Pope. He guaranteed freedom of worship, took away the church's right to tithes, shut down seven hundred monasteries, sold their land, stated that marriage was "a civil contract", had services shortened and rewritten and cut out a whole lot of Holy Days.

He outraged Pope Pius VI so much that he paid Joseph a visit. Joseph was extremely polite to him, assured him he was a good Catholic and was simply smartening the religion up a bit. He suggested the Pope should really think about doing the same once he got home. He held a banquet for his visitor and then sent the Pope off back to Rome; the poor befuddled man having achieved nothing.

Joseph abolished the death penalty and ended censorship of the press and theatre, none of which edicts lasted long after his death. He created a sort of Domesday Book (Old English, heaven knows what it is in old German) so he would know how much tax everyone should pay.

He offered higher education to a small number of boys and girls and even created scholarships for poor children, and actually came up with the money. He tried to centralize medical care by building a large hospital, the Alleman's Krankenhaus, which didn't turn out to be such a good idea as it also centralised diseases and an epidemic broke out with twenty per cent of the people dying. However, his actions did ensure that Vienna in later years would become a preeminent city in the field of medicine.

Under Joseph, religious tolerance was the best in Europe for many centuries. In 1789, he issued a charter for the Jews, abolishing communal autonomy and enabling the Jews to control their own affairs. He made an edict that everyone should speak German. The Hungarians took great exception to that. So perhaps just to annoy them, he took away the Hungarian Royal Crown and wouldn't let them join in his coronation. They did get the crown back in 1790.

One of the measures enforced by him was to create a type of secret police, the Obrigkeit, much like the East German secret police during the communist regime, which he instigated to ensure that he knew what everyone was doing all the time. People were terrified of them.

Despite all the good things he did, the ordinary people weren't happy; they didn't like the way he interfered in every part of their lives. Old customs were pushed aside, and to be suddenly told, "We're not doing that anymore", unsettled them. People deserted him and he died a sad and lonely man at the age of forty-six, feeling he had achieved nothing and that he was unloved.

Joseph was succeeded by his brother, Leopold, who had always been incredibly jealous of Joseph, and had just been waiting for a chance to take over and undo practically all the good things Joseph had done (except for the secret police; they were too entrenched and there was no getting rid of them. Of course, they may not have been a good thing).

CHAPTER 36

George III and the Prince Regent

George III was extremely dull but kind, kindness being a rare thing in a king.

He was a family man with no interest in taking lovers. He affectionate to his children and enjoyed every aspect of family life. From a young age he had weird turns that appear to have been the result of porphyria or he may have been bipolar. He was he able to take an interest in running the country only in his earlier years when he was sane and helped by his Prime Minister, Pitt the Younger (imagine being called "Pitt the Younger" all the time).

When his periods of sanity grew fewer and fewer, something had to be done. The king would have much preferred Pitt the Younger to have the responsibility, but Parliament disagreed. The first Regency Bill was passed in 1789, authorising the Prince of Wales to act as regent. He had limited powers, however, because the king kept coming good and was far more interested in affairs of state than his son.

Despite his health problem, George III was one of the more sensible monarchs, who took a deep interest in the government. When the Tories, led by Charles Fox - who the king thought was an odious man - wanted to grant the East India Company rights over how India should govern itself, George informed the House of Lords that any of its peers who thought about voting for such a move would be from then on considered his implacable foe. Needless to say, the Bill wasn't passed and everything was back in the Whig camp under Pitt the Younger and against the Prince Regent and Charles Fox.

I didn't realise until I was reading about the Prince Regent how heavily Oliver Cromwell had come down on the Catholics. It was nearly as bad as being Jewish, except they didn't actually get thrown out of the country. All I ever knew was a Catholic couldn't be King or Queen, nor could any member of the royal family marry a Catholic without giving up their right to the throne. There was a whole heap of other stuff. They couldn't own land, be in the army, go to university, except apparently if you were one of the Dukes of Norfolk. (They did have a minor setback in Elizabeth's regain when the Duke had his head chopped off, but they got their dukedom back with Charles II.) Perhaps they had a sort of get-out of jail free card clause because they certainly owned land and cropped up in various goings-on with the government. Attempts were made to repeal the Catholic Act while King George was alive, but he wouldn't have a bar of it. Pitt the Younger lost out to the Tories over it.

The king must have been a very tranquil soul or perhaps deaf. When someone took a shot at him while he was at the theatre (a crack pot, with no political motive), the king took a chance to have a nap in the interval once things were under control.

It was in this period that, having lost the American colonies, Britain decided to look around for somewhere to put their unwanted criminals and Australia came into play.

Finally, in 1811, the king lost his marbles completely and the Prince Regent took over. He wasn't particularly interested in the running of the country but he did enjoy having things named after him. Thus we got Regent Street, Regent's Park, Regents Canal and the pavilion in Brighton. He loved to design uniforms for himself; dressing up was rather a favourite way of spending his time. One of his closest friends was Beau Brummell, a dandy who influenced the entire ton (the top 400 of the day) as to how they should dress, wash and clean their teeth. He stopped men wearing the most extraordinary wigs, painting their faces and wearing high-heeled shoes, and achieved great improvement all round. The only trouble was that he didn't have much money and if you want to play with the rich and famous, however you go about it, it generally ends up costing money. The Prince Regent got annoyed with him, for whatever reason, and cut him dead at a party, which pushed Brummell into uttering the famous words, "Who's your fat friend?", and that was the end of his life as a leader of fashion. He died in poverty and, some say, insane - probably from not having facilities to bathe and clean his teeth.

The prince was, however, very good to his family and also to any French émigrés who found their way to England. He found them places to live and provided money to live on.

Despite being told he couldn't, he married divorcee Maria Fitzherbert, a Catholic, in a secret civil ceremony, which was declared invalid. As everyone pointed out, she could not become queen and he needed an heir. If they had gone out of their way to find someone who really didn't suit an effete young man, precious in his ways, they couldn't have done better than produce Caroline of Brunswick. She was loud, uncouth and rarely - very rarely - washed.

The marriage lasted until she produced a baby princess (although he didn't divorce her). It would have been absurd to say, " I'm divorcing you because you don't wash and are too loud". He was quite happy with Mrs. Fitzherbert and simply ignored Caroline, not allowing her to attend his coronation when he became King (George IV) in 1820. For some reason, the people loved Caroline and really didn't care for the new king at all. They thought he spent too much money on himself and bragged about his achievements (which were virtually nil). He loved to pretend he was a real soldier. He followed the Napoleonic wars and was forever telling everybody how he won the battle of Waterloo, quite often in front of Wellington, who politely pointed out "But Your Highness, you weren't there."

CHAPTER 37

The French Revolution

Marie Antoinette was one of those people who could sit still and life fell on her. She was not the brightest pebble of the beach and at twelve could not read or write in either French or German, but she had a sweet disposition, and was very pretty and elegant. At fifteen she was married to the Dauphin of France, Louis XVI, who was equally dim (though not as pretty). When she did not become pregnant for the first few years of her marriage, the blame, of course, was laid on her. Various doctors poked and prodded her until one said, "Oh, for God sake, has anyone checked him?" (only in French). Louis was examined and his foreskin removed, and from then on there was no problem. He fathered seven children with Marie, and who knows how many elsewhere?

In the beginning, the French thought Marie lovely, as they always liked pretty things, but as the years wore on and the people became more discontent, the Queen's reputation became tarnished by gossip. The feelings against her were "bought to a head by the affair of the necklace": Before his death, Louis XV had ordered a diamond necklace for his then mistress, Madam Du Barry. It had to be of the best quality available (but was, in fact, large and clunky). This may have been a lovely idea in theory, however quite stupid in practice, especially when the country was literarily broke. Unfortunately, Louis died while the necklace was being made, and it was then offered to Marie Antoinette, who having never said a sensible thing in her life, suddenly came up with, "I don't want it; they'd be better off spending the money on equipping a man-of-war".

The necklace popped up again when a woman with a long name, Jeanne de Valois-Saint-Remy, thought she had found a good way of earning herself some money. The lady happened to be the mistress of Cardinal de Rohan, who Marie Antoinette really didn't like. Jeanne persuaded the cardinal that she was a friend of the queen, and as the queen actually didn't want this extremely ugly piece of jewellery, he could offer to buy it and give it to her and thus get himself in the queen's good books. It was real soap opera material with maids - and, at one stage, a prostitute - dressing up as the queen and meeting with co-conspirators in dark places, etc. During all this intrigue, Jeanne forged Marie's signature on an order to buy the necklace. It all ended in tears with those concerned being found guilty, but everyone blamed the queen, who'd had nothing to do with it. Marie became more unpopular, and it is believed that the whole matter served as kindling for the French Revolution.

The French Revolution doesn't make much sense to me. People usually revolt against religion strictures or other counties, but the French seem to have had a revolution because there was no one in charge. The place was broke, the people in Paris were starving, the intellectuals didn't like the aristocrats, and the diamond necklace affair didn't help. No one was keen on the Protestants, but there was no one there to say, "Okay now, stop. This is what we're going to do." If it was anyone's fault it was Louis XIV's. He had sown the seeds by building Versailles and making everyone come and live with him. He then had further delusions of grandeur and kept starting wars, which he inevitably lost along with colonies in America, Canada and India. Poor Louis XVI, who wouldn't hurt a fly, inherited a country which was stony broke and full of people who had nothing to eat. It was a tinder box but, no, Marie didn't say "Let them eat cake".

You had a group of intellectuals arguing about what should be done, but coming up with nothing, apart from kill all the aristocrats. There was a whole bunch of them, but Robespierre, Talleyrand and Marat are the only three that come to mind. They guillotined Robespierre, and Marat got stabbed in the bath by his mistress. Talleyrand seemed to stick around.

On July 14th 1790, the people of Paris decided to free the prisoners in the Bastille. I'm sure the seven people who were in there must have been delighted. However, including the prisoners there were other items in the prison, including guns, gunpowder and all kinds of armaments. So, here we have a lot of angry people running around with guns. As they didn't actually want to kill each other, the next best thing they could think of was capturing and guillotining any aristocrat they could get their hands on. People were terrified and fled in all directions. With the aid of Austria, the king and queen plus their children and a couple of other people made plans for their escape and managed to get away. Unfortunately, the king left all the details of the plan on his bed (and this was the person everyone thought was devious and going to do appalling things to the country). All he needed was a nanny and a minister who could take charge. Of course, they were all captured having a leisurely lunch and brought back to Paris. Louis XVI and Marie Antoinette were guillotined.

The Royalist were fighting the Revolutionaries, who were fighting those who wanted to abolish religion, who were against the moderates, who just wanted peace and quiet. Until finally someone came along who thought "This mess has got to stop!".

CHAPTER 38

Napoleon

Napoleon was one of those people, like Cher, Sting or Mozart, who appear to need only the one name. Of course, he had a second one, which was Bonaparte, but everyone now knows him simply by the name "Napoleon". (Conversely, in his own time, people more often referred to him as "Bonaparte".)

When I started writing this I thought "What do I know about him?". Only that he was this awful person who tried to take over Europe, and in all of his portraits he always seemed to have his right hand stuck inside his jacket, for some reason.

However, after reading about Napoleon I found him rather sweet in many ways, even though he did manage to kill an awful lot of people. But then Wellington killed quite a few too.

Napoleon was born in Corsica where his father was serving as the ambassador for France and he trained early on to be a gunner in the French army. When the revolution broke out, England, Austria and Spain all attacked France. Napoleon, who had recently arrived from Corsica, found himself fighting against his fellow Frenchmen. The king came out to talk to his people, but was booed and he scuttled back indoors again and Napoleon learnt a lesson which he never forgot. He said to his brother "If he had come out on horseback waving a sword, the day would have been his. There has always got to be leadership." When he refused to fight against his fellow Frenchmen, he was sent him to Toulon where his commanding officer was General Carteauz, who in private life had been the court painter - of course, excellent choice for an army general.

Napoleon decided, quite reasonably, that the general knew nothing about warfare, and so took charge, especially after Carteauz managed to blow up their largest gun. Napoleon was trained as a gunner and knew what he doing. He organised guns from all over the place, built parapets and blazed away. He was wounded but not too badly and in two days he had subdued the town.

Britain's Admiral Lord Hood set fire to all the French ships he could and then hightailed it out of there. Napoleon was promoted to brigadier-general. He ran around trying to bring some law and order into things and managed to get the revolution on a stable footing and became a general. Then he met a woman whose name was Rose, but Napoleon didn't care for that so he changed it to "Josephine" and married her before he set off on his next foray. He had this annoying habit throughout his life - if he didn't like something, he'd change it (which must have upset a great many people along the way).

The next thing he had to do was sort out Italy, which was a whole bunch of small principalities, who were always fighting with one another and anyone else they felt got in their way. The army Napoleon had inherited was a messy affair. Its soldiers were half-starved and many of them didn't have shoes. He spent most of his money on getting them fed and properly clothed. Then, off he went to sort out Italy. The main cities being Milan, which the Austrians had, and Piedmonte, which had a king, Victor Amadeus III, who was apparently very vain, and had imprisoned any liberals who came his way and reinstated the Inquisition. Charming man. He had a habit of falling asleep so they nicknamed him "King of the Dormice". While he was having a nap he possibly missed many chances to decapitate someone or burn then at the stake.

The French powers-that-be also wanted Napoleon to get rid of the Pope. It didn't take him long to get the whole lot sorted out, but when it came to the Pope he found an old man, exhausted from years of trying to keep the unruly countries and states from killing each other. Napoleon told him "Don't worry, everything's under control now, so you just go back to being Pope and doing Pope things and I'll handle the rest."

Napoleon apparently won his battles because he didn't fight his wars like a gentleman. Because he was a gunner; he used his men as though they were guns. Being from Corsica where there were virtually no roads, he had grown up with an eye for topography. I don't know why this should be important but apparently it is in warfare. He was fighting the Austrians, but at the same time he was liberating the Italians. He announced, "People of Italy, the French army has come to break your chains. We shall respect your property, your religion and your customs."

This is not a man who was vicious nor a barbarian. Although he did kill far too many people, his basic plan was sound, but by then Napoleon had become someone to fear. He had the army behind him and was virtually the toughest character in town. He considered invading England but became distracted and didn't follow through. The powers-that-be thought that if he was not going to have a go at England, how about tackling Egypt? They thought he may have some trouble with Malta, which as an island had never been defeated. He asked why and was told by everyone, "Well, it's never has been defeated." He sat and wondered about this for a while then sent a couple of spies to see what exactly was going on in Malta. They discovered the Grand Master was an elderly gentleman, who capitulated as soon as it was explained to him that if he didn't, they would blow him out of the water.

Napoleon got quite excited about going to Egypt. Apart from blocking the British route to India, by going there he could begin collecting around him an assortment of scientists, medical personnel, technologists, artists and mathematicians. What he didn't want was to start a fight with the Turks, and he organized with Talleyrand, the French Foreign Minister, to go to Turkey and negotiate a peace treaty, which Talleyrand naturally forgot to do.

Napoleon was able to march his troops into Alexandra because someone had forgotten to shut one of the gates. The Mamelukes, the slave soldiers who ruled Egypt, had never seen heavy guns and dived into the Nile to flee from them. Arriving in Cairo, Napoleon discovered some fine mosques and the Mamelukes' palace, but the rest of the place was just a collection of hovels and bazaars. Having looked around and moved into the palace, the next thing he knew was that Nelson had blown up his fleet in the Nile, and he had no way of getting out. Most people would have a least stopped and thought, "Oh my God, what am I going to do now?" Napoleon immediately said "This is wonderful! I'll have more time to sort out the Egyptians and explore."

He read the Koran and wandered around telling everyone what a great book it was, and that every Frenchman was a Muslim. That was until an Imam told him that if indeed he was a Muslim, he'd better get himself circumcised and stop drinking wine! Napoleon thought for a moment and said, "In my heart, I am a Muslim."

He also discovered the ancient stream that later became the Suez Canal. He did a whole lot of work on it, but decided that to complete it would be far too expensive because for some reason they thought it would need locks to operate it, so they just put it on the back burner.

He did one thing he did which was possibly the most important act of his whole career: he discovered the Rosetta Stone which unlocked the hieroglyphics and made the Egyptians aware of themselves as a people with a great past. Until then no one had been able to decipher the hieroglyphics and it took Napoleon's group of code breakers and scientists with the help of the Rosetta Stone to discover how important Egypt had been to the ancient world. He set up schools, and the numerous medical and scientific improvements he made marked the foundation of the modern-day Egypt.

After reading about him, Napoleon seems to have been a much nicer man than I realized. His plan was to make Europe united, a bit like the Common Market. He crowned himself emperor in 1804 and made Josephine empress. He divorced her in 1810 because he wanted children - which she hadn't been able to give him - and she spent far too much money. There was much crying and he never really got over her, but he married Marie Louise of Austria, who presented him with a son.

With all fighting and taking things over, he was really getting up the noses of the British, Austrians and the Russians. At this point, the British had two men who were as clever at warfare as Napoleon (they had also been learning from what he did in some of his previous battles), Horatio Nelson and Arthur Wellesley (better known as the Duke Of Wellington). I don't know about the Russians and Austrians, but the British navy was the best in the world, and Nelson defeated him at the Battle of Trafalgar, which fought off the coast of Spain. During this battle Nelson lost his life on 21 October, 1805. For years it was national holiday in Great Britain, and one of the few dates I actually remember.

Napoleon's next mistake was to attack Russia. He forgot that nobody in their right mind makes a full blown attack on Russia - maybe nibble at the edges a bit, but a full-blown attack was lunacy. It's too big to get home in time for winter, because as we know one never fights in winter, and winter in Russia is really horrible.

As Napoleon's troops advanced towards Moscow, the Russians ducked and weaved, and eventually just before entering Moscow they had a big fight, which the French actually won. It was a terrible battle, very bloody. Neither side had ever been in anything so horrible.

Napoleon had a methodical mind and had no idea he was about to come across the Russian mind, which was much more complex and anything but methodical. They would prefer to burn their city to the ground rather than let Napoleon win. He marched into Moscow, expecting Alexander to give in but instead found a city in ruins, a total scorched earth policy. He could not conceive that anyone would do something that to his mind was so totally bizarre. The French had to make their way back in the Russian winter and that finished them, especially with the Cossacks nipping at their heels. He eventually got back to France with about a third of his army. Finally, the powers that be back in Paris decided that infuriating the world was not so good for France after all, and turned against Napoleon. He abdicated in favour of his son.

The British sent him to Elba, telling him he could be Emperor of Elba if he wanted to. At first he was very depressed and even tried to kill himself, but then pulled himself together and started to reorganise Elba in terms of rearranging its education system, medical and scientific infrastructure. He even amassed a small army and navy. Having done all this, he got bored and escaped the island.

Meanwhile, back in France, the Bourbons were back in favour, and Louis XVII's brother, who had always been jealous of Louis, had taken over as king. He married Maria Giuseppina of Savoy, whom he couldn't stand. He found her repulsive. Apparently, she never washed or cleaned her teeth Mind you, he wasn't such a great catch either. He was obese and waddled everywhere.

As Louis XVII didn't have any children for a long time into he reign, his brother was determined to beat him at producing progeny, so despite his dislike of his wife he managed to get her pregnant twice, but both times she miscarried. (Antonia Fraser, who wrote about him, for some reason, thought he was impotent, but apparently not.)

Then back came Napoleon, and everybody rushed to greet him with great joy, including Marshal Ney, who had promised to be faithful to the king. Marshal Bernadotte, another of Napoleon's soldiers, ended up as King of Sweden. (That I have never understood but then I have never understood how half the Kings, Queens and Emperors ended up in the positions they did.)

It turned out that the people disliked their fat king and much preferred Napoleon, so the unpopular Louis XVII fled to Belgium. When he eventually returned, fighting erupted once more. There was battle after battle, and most of them Napoleon won, until they finally ended up in Belgium for the Battle of Waterloo. It was very strange affair as many of the officers brought their wives along to watch the battle, and before it the Duchess of Richmond threw a ball. After the ball was over, there were scenes of tearful wives bidding their husbands goodbye as the men headed into battle. It was Wellington, with the help of someone called Marshal Blucher, who won the day.

The British got hold of Napoleon and had him transferred to St Helena, where he died in May 1821. His tomb stands alone at Les Invalides in Paris. The tomb was part a project originally initiated by Louis XIV. I don't think he would have been at all pleased with Napoleon resting there.

Between 1814-15 The Congress of Vienna - chaired by Austria's Metternich - was formed to try to settle what actually had happened with all these European wars. Looking at it from a couple of hundred years away, most of what had happened wasn't in fact bad, certainly the countries Napoleon had invaded were better off and far more organized once he'd got through with them (except of course for Italy, but it would take an act of God to get them organised). The delegates of the congress were never all there at the same time. They mostly only popped in when they weren't fighting other people. The main participants were Austria, Prussia, Britain and Sweden. Their goal was to restore the old boundaries. What they actually achieved was to undo a lot of the good things Napoleon had done. Smaller states got swallowed up by the larger ones, and the congress was criticized for suppressing emerging states.

Henry Kissinger wrote that the congress was "a deliberate attempt to undercut the first genuine attempt to create an international order base." Napoleon was responsible for overthrowing feudalism in western Europe, liberating property laws, closing Jewish ghettos (although they returned pretty soon after he died), ending the Inquisition (which also came back), reduced the power of the Church and proclaiming equality for all men. It was a pity he had to have all those battles - and cause the deaths of so many people - to achieve what he did.

CHAPTER 39

Josephine

Josephine was born in Martinique, but the family moved to France when their estate where they grew sugar was destroyed by a hurricane. There, Rose (as her name was then) married a minor aristocrat, Alexander de Beauharnais. They had two children: Hortense and Eugene. Hortense ended up marrying Napoleon's brother, Louis.

The marriage to Alexander doesn't appear to have been a very happy one, and then the poor man was arrested by the revolutionaries and eventually guillotined. Even Rose was interned, but was released after a few months. One thing her jailers found extraordinary was the way she looked after her cell, she cleaned it out every day and kept everything spotless.

Rose was a great partygoer, who loved to gossip and have people over for a drink. She had affairs with several men, and then she met Napoleon, who fell wildly in love with her, though she was a little older: he was 26, she was 32. She found all this devotion slightly startling, but when he asked her to marry him, she thought, "Well, why not? Nothing much else is happening."

Napoleon didn't care for the name Rose, so changed it to Josephine. After about two days of honeymooning, he was off to sort out Italy. His newly-named wife very soon got bored and started running around with a handsome young hussar named Hippolyte Charles. When Napoleon learned of this, he was determined to divorce her, and wrote her fuming letters. Nelson captured the ship carrying the letters, read them, thought them extremely funny and sent them off to be published in Paris. Napoleon was deeply embarrassed. To save himself further public humiliation, he dismissed all thoughts of divorcing Josephine, though he did start having affairs himself.

Josephine was kind and sweet, but she was not, shall we say, good with money. She bought an incredibly expensive house and furnished it beautifully, but the furniture tended to be delicate and not very practical. When Napoleon got back, he exploded, "You've spent far too much money, and I know it looks very elegant, but there's nowhere to sit!"

At his coronation Napoleon crowned himself, having obviously come to the conclusion that if you want something done well, do it yourself, and then he crowned his spend-thrift wife Empress of France. Whatever Napoleon did, he couldn't seem to make her understand she should be frugal with money. In desperation, he went to his minister of finance to get him to talk to her: "But whatever you do, don't make her cry".

Eventually, it became obvious that Josephine was not going to produce the longed-for heir, and when Josephine's grandson, Napoleon Louis Charles, eldest son of Hortense and Louis, died of croup at the age of four, Napoleon began to look round in earnest for someone to give him a child. He explained to Josephine that he needed an heir, and so had to divorce her and remarry. Much crying on both sides occurred, and finally Josephine moved into the house that Napoleon had been so furious with her for buying and turned it into a thing of great beauty. The gardens were quite extraordinary, with several greenhouses where she grew pineapples and oranges, and her roses were the prize of Europe. She even had one officially named after her. She continued to be as social as always and had a great many visitors, including Napoleon, who never really got over her. When she died in 1810, he shut himself away for more that a week and wouldn't see or speak to anyone.

Josephine's legacy went much further than a pretty house and a lovely garden. Her grandson from her daughter Hortense, became Napoleon

II. Her son Eugene's daughter married the King of Sweden. He himself was the Duke of Lichtenberg, and one of his sons married into the Russian Royal family. So the end, Josephine was not just some dalliance of Napoleon's but a significant person in her own right, leaving her mark on many royal families in Europe.

CHAPTER 40

Lady Hamilton and Nelson

In writing about them, you can't really separate Lady Hamilton and Nelson unless you have some deep interest in naval battles (which I don't). Nelson was fascinating. He was quite small and in his early life he married Francis Nesbit, a widow from a small island in the Caribbean.

Really, the only bits that interest me about Nelson (apart from the fact he kept getting himself badly damaged in the various battles he took part in) are those that involve Lady Hamilton. She started life as a housemaid, then came to London, changed her name to Emma Hart and was working at Drury Lane as a dresser for the actors, where she came across Sir Harry Featheronehaugh, pronounced "Fanshaw". (Sometimes the English are very strange. Only the English can take a name like Warwick and pronounce it "Warrick", or Reading, pronounced "Reding", Teignmouth pronounced "Tinmuth", and Cholmondeley, pronounced - wait for it - "Chumlee. There are tons of them!)

Anyway, Harry took a liking to her and brought her back to his family home, Uppark, where he kept her as a sort of family pet to perform for his male friends. As they sat around and drank, do a she would little dance on the table top, slowly taking off more and more clothes (an early bit of burlesque-type strip-tease?).

On a whim, Charles Greville, second son of the 1st Earl of Warwick (pronounced "Warrick", remember), brought Emma to London and proceeded to educate her to be a lady. He got slightly bored with her when she became become pregnant (probably to Featheronehaugh, pronounced - oh, never mind!) and so sent her to live with her grandmother in Wales until after the birth. The child was fostered out at Greville's insistence, and Emma returned to London, where George Romney, the painter, discovered her and was obsessed with having her pose for him. She did her little dances for him, without taking her clothes off. He dressed her up in all sorts of outfits and taught her how to pose. The portraits sold like hot cakes. She became like an eighteenth-century Kardashian (that is, she was famous for having her picture everywhere).

Charles became irritated with trailing around after the, by then, famous Emma. He was very short of cash and was desperate to get a rich wife, and he had always thought of Emma as a kind of plaything to be discarded after his interest had waned. So, when his uncle, William Hamilton, arrived from Naples and fell for Emma, Greville did a deal to sell her to his uncle. The agreement was that when William died, he would leave Greville his money and his property in Wales.

It was arranged for Emma to go for a little holiday to Naples, where Sir William happened to be the British Ambassador. It took a little while for it to dawn on Emma that she was not going back. She was furious, and wrote a letter to Charles telling him to be very careful or she would marry his uncle and so inherit his money. Greville didn't believe this as he had the agreement with his uncle.

However, Emma did marry Sir William, blissfully unaware that this would leave her without any security. However, as Lady Hamilton she did become quite famous in her own right. People liked Emma and she became firm friends with the Queen of Naples, Maria Carol, who was another of Maria Therese's daughters (who were scattered around Europe in various royal households). Emma became extremely popular for the portraits that were known as "Emma's Attitudes". It was the thing to be to invited to one of Emma's soirees where she would perform her "Attitudes". She paraded in various costumes, striking poses of the sort she had learnt from Romney.

Nelson sailed into port after having lost an eye at Calva during the battles for Corsica. He was hailed a great hero. Emma cooed and fussed over him, nursing him back to health.

The next time he arrived in Naples was five years later after having lost his right arm in the Battle of Santa Cruz de Tenerife, and was feeling not at all well. By now he had achieved rock-star status. Emma again nursed him, never leaving his side. Although she had begun to get fat, she still had her pretty face and Nelson adored her, and not only because of all the attention she lavished on him; he really fell in love with her.

As the French army was making its way towards Naples, Nelson got the royal family, and Sir William and Emma out just in time. (He did this without seeking permission from the British government, but as Nelson and Lady Hamilton were possibly the two most famous people in Britain at the time, all was forgiven.) Unfortunately, on the voyage there was a dreadful storm during which the young Prince of Naples died in Emma's arm.

In the same storm, the ship carrying all Sir William's treasures was sunk. Sir William was a collector of Greek and Roman antiquities, and had most of his money tied up in them. Thus, almost his fortune was lost. In a somewhat strange arrangement, he, Emma and Nelson all lived together in a house in Piccadilly, along with Emma's mother.

Nelson divorced his wife in 1801, and he and Emma had a daughter they named Horatia. By this stage, Sir William was far from well, and sat quietly by as the three of them trundled around the British countryside being admired by one and all. To get Nelson away from Emma, the British government (who were not quite as enamoured of her as the public were), sent him back to sea. Sir William died in 1803, leaving Emma eight hundred pounds a year, while all the properties he left to Greville were heavily mortgaged. So, Emma got the best of the deal, after all.

Nelson and Emma continued to live together, although everyone was somewhat scandalised at their obviously intimate relationship. By now

Emma was really chubby, but she had a very sweet nature and was kind, so when people got to know her, they found that they rather liked her.

Nelson was made "The Most Noble Lord Horatio Nelson, Viscount, Baron of the Nile", and various other titles that other countries had bestowed on him. They lived happily in a country house, with Nelson popping off to battle every so often. And then came Trafalgar, a battle fought off the coast of Spain. There, on the 21st October 1805, while strolling on the deck of the ship, Victory, Nelson was shot through the spine by an enemy sharp-shooter. He knew he was dying and uttered the immortal words "Kiss me, Hardy" (he was obviously rather fond of the ship's captain), and apparently begged everyone in sight to look after Emma. When he finally died, they pickled him in a barrel of brandy. When the Victory arrived at Greenwich he was placed in a lead-lined coffin and taken to the Admiralty and from there to St. Paul's where he was buried in a sarcophagus meant for Cardinal Wolseley. So, things do come in useful if you keep them long enough. In his will, apart from everything else, he bequeathed Emma to the nation.

Bequest to the Nation

The nation wasn't in the slightest bit interested in having Emma bequeathed to it. Although everyone felt Nelson may well be England's greatest hero, Emma (to them) was a slightly common woman, who had once been beautiful but had now become fat and uninteresting, and as far as they were concerned she could just fade away (though Terrance Rattigan got a good play out of it all).

Nelson's brother came in for all the glory, the title and everything, while Emma spent some time in prison for debt, and then moved to France where she died of amoebae dysentery in 1815. However, she would always be remembered for Romney's paintings, and her love affair with Nelson

CHAPTER 41

Princess Charlotte

Having got his wife pregnant the Prince Regent (George, Prince of Wales, later King George IV), would have nothing further to do with her. When a daughter, Princess Charlotte, was born in 1796, he would not allow the child to live with her mother, nor did he particularly want a small baby crying around him, so she grew up in her own establishment, being allowed to see her mother on the odd occasion the prince was feeling mellow. As she reached marriageable age her father wanted her to marry William of Orange. (His last marriage had worked out so well.)

The girl didn't like him, and wanted to marry Prince Leopold of Saxe Coburg Saalfeld (another of those extraordinary names the German principalities had). The general public also didn't care for Prince William; he was referred to as "Silly Willie". After a whole lot of grumbling on all sides and much debate in parliament, where they tended to bicker rather than find an outcome, the princess wrote to her favourite uncle, Augustus Duke of Sussex, telling him she was over eighteen and should be allowed to marry whomever she pleased. He raised it in parliament and everyone was delighted that a solution had been found, a Bill was passed in favour of Charlotte marrying Prince Leopold. The Prince Regent never spoke to his brother again.

Queen Caroline tended to have affairs with various men, which annoyed those in power because she wasn't exactly subtle. She tired of the peevishness and was becoming fed up with England. While many found her amusing and far more pleasant than the Regent Prince, the general census was that she should go and live somewhere else. She quite agreed. When told her mother was leaving the country, Princess Charlotte shrugged and said, "Oh really?". Her mother left and they never saw one another again.

The princess married her chosen prince, and when she became pregnant eighteen months later everyone was overjoyed, but the poor girl died in childbirth, taking the child with her. She was twenty-one. There was a stunned and awful silence as the whole country mourned. Then the realisation - what on earth were they going to do about an heir to the throne? The Prince Regent was happily settled back again with his mistress, Mrs. Fitzherbert, and had no intention of looking for another wife. He had several brothers, all middle-aged and happily living with women they loved; none of them had any wish to go hunting for a suitable princess to marry. "Well, one of us has to get married and produce an heir", said the family. "The people have only just got used to us. We can't expect parliament to go searching around for another German family to take over. One of you has got to marry someone suitable."

The Prince Regent stormed about, as did parliament. Everyone went into a frenzy looking for suitable wives. They sent the younger brother, Adolphus Duke of Cambridge, on a fishing expedition to see what he could come up with. He returned with Princess Augusta of Hesse-Kassel, and then when no one wanted her, he married her himself. The poor woman must have been most confused.

Finally, Prince Edward, Duke of Kent and the fourth son of King George III, reluctantly married Princess Victoria Saxe-Coburg-Saalfeld, a very disagreeable women, but she did produce Victoria, so the succession was secure.

CHAPTER 42

King William IV

Prince William, the Duke of Clarence, lived happily for many years with an Irish actress called Dorothea Jordan and had ten illegitimate children by her, all living, and all with the surname FitzClarence. (The word Fitz simple means 'son of', but at this time it usually indicated an illegitimate child of a nobleman.)

(Speaking of names, in the great aristocratic families of Great Britain the children tend to end up with different titles. Take the Bedford family. Years ago, I used to know Rudy Russell, the second son of the Duke of Bedford. He was Lord Rudolph Russell, while his older brother Robin was the Marquess of Tavistock, and then came their father The Duke of Bedford; all the titles making the connection of their family name seem to disappear.)

Pressed to provide an heir for the throne, Prince William finally left his beloved actress and married Princess Adelaide of Saxe Meiningen, but as he had no living children with her, the duty then fell to his brother Edward, Duke of Kent, who married possibly the bossiest woman in the world, Victoria of Saxe-Coburg-Salted (yet another weird German place name). They had a daughter, Victoria, in 1820, the same year that George III died, and finally the Prince Regent ascended to the throne. As Prince Regent, he had been a minor nuisance who ran up enormous debts. As king, he was far worse. He meddled in politics, about which he didn't appear to have much grasp. Then, fortunately - as far as the country was concerned - he died in 1830.

The next in line of the brothers was the Duke of Clarence, who came to the throne as William IV. William IV was much more organised than his brother. He had served in the navy when he was younger and had quite a clear idea of what was happening in the world. He was the last British king to choose his own Prime Minister. It was under his watch that Lord Melbourne first appeared. "Sailor Billy", as the king was known, was involved in the American War of Independence. While he was in New York, serving with the navy, there was a plot to kidnap him, until Admiral Digby pointed out to the plotters what a very bad idea this was, as it would bring down the Wrath of God on them, so they gave up the idea.

William saw through several good parliamentary acts. He abolished slavery in 1833. Denmark had abolished it in 1803 (somehow, I don't see Denmark mixed up with something as cruel as slavery, after their turn at being Vikings they seemed to calm down and become very civilized).

William, tried yet again to sort out what the Catholics could and could not do. He also tried to sell Buckingham Palace, buy nobody wanted it. Like most of his family, he had a slightly eccentric streak. He was made Lord High Admiral until he decided to take the entire fleet out for a run, or whatever you do with ships, without telling anyone. This caused major conniptions throughout the country as no one knew where he was or what he was doing. He arrived back not having taken over any small countries, chopped off anyone's ear, slaughtered a dog, or even tried to annex Poland. He just went for a sail with all his old chums. The government decided perhaps it was safest if he wasn't an admiral any more, just king. He did do away with the cat-o-nine-tails (a very good thing).

William, like everyone else, strongly disliked his sister-in-law, the Duchess of Kent, Victoria's mother. She was Victoria's guardian and told everyone in sight that it was so. (It's amazing how powerful women often have very bossy mothers.) William went round telling everyone he would make it his business not to die until Victoria had gained her full age of eighteen, as then she could make her own decisions and not have that wretched woman meddling.

With many tiny villages merging into large towns because of the industrial revolution, it suddenly occurred to people they should have the right to vote. For hundreds of years places designated as Boroughs were allowed to choose members of parliament. The Boroughs could be large or consist of a few people living in a house 'with a hearth to boil a pot'. Only in England could something so weird have gone on working with no one say, "Hold on a minute, what are we doing here?".

The Duke of Norfolk (he does pop up, doesn't he?) had eleven Boroughs to his name, so he could basically put anyone he liked into parliament. Burgeoning towns such as Manchester, which had grown from a tiny village into a thriving metropolis, had no Boroughs of their own, so no one there had the right to vote. Parliament tried to sort it out. Whigs and Tories fought. Parliament was dissolved; there was rioting in the streets, and eventually Charles Grey, the Earl of Howick - Earl Grey tea is named after him - got the thing through.

Things calmed down, but this didn't seem to make a great deal of difference; they still had what they called "rotten boroughs" (that is, corrupt), such as those owned by the Duke of Norfolk and various chums. One town, Dunwich, had apparently fallen into the sea and didn't exist any more, but still had thirty votes. From 1832 parliament slowly got the mess into some sort of order. Even in the twentieth century there were still boroughs around that were known as "safe seats".

Parliament had to also sort out the Corn Laws. A tariff had been put on imported corn in the sixteenth century to keep corn prices high to favour domestic producers, but now people were disgruntled with the high food prices. The tariff was finally repealed in 1846 by the then Prime Minster, Sir Robert Peel. Much of parliament's time had been spent arguing whether they should or shouldn't repeal the damned thing. As Lord Melbourne said, as they came out of a five-hour discussion, "Well, gentlemen remind me, are we putting the price of bread up or down?"

CHAPTER 43

A Few Things I Find Odd and/or Entertaining

The Cato Conspiracy in 1820 was a group of people who wanted to assassinate the Prime Minister and do away with parliament. They were all caught within a couple of days. Some where sent to Australia, but five of them were sentenced to be hanged, drawn and quartered. (This had been fairly commonplace in the Middle Ages. First you hanged the person, almost to death, emasculated, disembowelled, chopped him into four pieces, and then to make sure he is quite dead, cut off his head. Charming.)

By the 1800s, hanging was still a great source of entertainment for the masses at the time (and that's were the term "Gallows Humour", comes from. If the person being hanged was able to make spectators laugh, the actual hanging was held off until he was no longer able to amuse the crowd. For example, one such prisoner supposedly examined the trapdoor and asked "Is it safe?".) So, the crowd settled down for a good series of hangings, but when the first man was quartered and his head chopped off, there was nearly a riot. People screamed, "What do you think you are doing? What are we barbarians?" The made it clear that hanging was all that was considered necessary, no quartering or chopping off of heads, thank you. The Government reflected on this and decided the crowd maybe right, but what to do with the head? They had planned to stick it on a post outside the Tower of London. Suddenly this didn't seem to be such a good idea. So, they stuck the person's head back on. What they did with the guts, I have no idea, but they buried him with the others, in an unmarked grave.

You may have wondered how large aristocratic families managed to keep intact with their big houses, their land and their money. It was all down to the concept of primogeniture. The eldest son - never the daughter - inherited the lot. Occasionally, the second son, if the mother had money of her own, got something.

The first son, if they were a political family went into politics. The second into the army, and the third into the church. God help anyone who came after that.

However, a shift in the order of things had begun to occur. A whole new section of society had cropped up that not only had money, but quite often more money that some of the aristocrats, who generally just had land and perhaps some buildings which were rented out for what was called a peppercorn rent, but not much else, except for their big house that took a lot of maintenance.

People view the eighteenth and early nineteenth century as very romantic (thanks to Barbara Cartland and sundry other writers), but think how boring it must have been. If you were poor, life must have been hell, and if you were rich, unless you were a soldier and there was a war on, you had servants who did everything for you. Sometimes politics interested them. (Two Prime Ministers actually had a duel over something quite trivial. On shot in the air and the other shot his opponent in the foot.) Gossip was very big, but the main source of entertainment was spending the weekend at each other's houses and having affairs with each other's spouses.

There were three main families of importance, the Bessboroughs, the Devonshires and the Lambs, who, as usual, came into different names once they gained their titles. They were deeply involved in politics. Lady Bessborough and the Duchess of Devonshire were sisters. Lady Bessborbough couldn't stand Lady Lamb. Many a political plot was hatched at weekend parties in their various houses at the weekend.

Promiscuity was rife. It was generally accepted that the first-born son was fathered by the husband but after that it was anyone's guess. Elizabeth, Viscountess Melbourne, was a typical example and when her first-born son died, no one had any idea who might be the father of her second son, William. Still, he came into the title of Lord Melbourne when his supposed father died.

William fell in love with Caroline, Lady Bessborough's daughter. Caroline looked like a little elf, frail and charming, but as mad as a hatter. To be honest, she was probably bipolar and today would have been medicated and become a rock star or something. But in the eighteenth and early nineteenth centuries she was a nightmare. She and William married before he came into his title. As he was still William Lamb, she became Caroline Lamb. He adored her and for a time they were happy. Then her eye fell on Byron, who had just written "Childe Harold's Pilgrimage", a long romantic poem, which made him immediately a star. Caroline decided she was madly in love with him, not considering that the poem was not the man. She threw herself at Byron and for a while it amused them both to flaunt society with their outrageous behaviour.

Caroline, who was born into "the ton" never imagined that society might throw her out. Byron was considered by the in crowd as interesting because of his poem. His personality, however, was far less flamboyant than Caroline's and he began to tire of the scandals she was causing. Caroline's husband, William, never for a moment considered the two of them were in love. He believed they were two quite brilliant people in their own way, using each other to stay in the limelight.

Byron wearying of the constant drama that surrounded them, wrote her a very cruel letter, basically telling her to go away. And when he snubbed her at a social gathering, she became hysterical, smashed a glass and started to frantically cut herself. This was the final straw as far as her family and most of society were concerned. She was taken away to the family home. William tried to stay with her, but it became virtually impossible to contain her outbursts of rage. She had to be locked away for her own and everybody's safety. She needed to be kept as quiet as possible. She did write a couple of books, which in their time were quite scandalous, and came up with the famous phrase about Byron: "He's mad, bad, and dangerous to know". She died fairly young and Lord Melbourne never re-married.

When he was very much older and serving as Prime Minister, he more or less fell in love with Queen Victoria. At the time of the accession to the throne he had to help her learn the ropes as it were. She was eighteen-year-old and looking for a father figure. He was there to guide her, spending four or five hours a day with her, and it wasn't until she married Albert that their partnership broke up, leaving him a very sad old man. As a Prime Minister he was a pretty cool guy and only he and Disraeli could be considered to be in the least interesting. Melbourne did have one great fault. He wasn't interested in bringing things to a conclusion, all he wanted to know was why they were there in the first place. This was one of the reasons the government argued for years about things that could have been done reasonably easily, such as the Corn Bill and deciding who should or shouldn't vote.

CHAPTER 44

The Rothschilds

The Rothschilds were another fascinating family. Mayer Rothschild handled the finances for the German Landgraves of Hesse-Kassel in the Free City of Frankfurt (Frankfurt was declared an Imperial Free City in 1372, making the city subordinate to the Holy Roman Emperor and not to a king or local noble). It was the second half of the eighteenth century, and times were changing. Thanks to the Industrial Revolution, there was a whole new class of people with money, people who needed to borrow more money to pay for sensible things such as building factories or railways, which would become profitable businesses. In fact, making a profit was their major concern; they had no interest in starting wars or upsetting the status quo.

Mayer Rothschild opened the first bank in Frankfurt. It was small but did very well, and - as there was no king to realise he owed more money to the bank than he could ever pay back - there was no reason for Mayer to be suddenly thrown out of the country. Banking was a solid business. Mayer had five sons, all with completely different personalities, but all trained in banking. They understood money and what you could or could not do with it.

Mayer decided he would open branches around the world. His eldest son, Amschel, he kept in Frankfurt with him. James, his youngest son, seemed far more sophisticated than the rest, so he sent him to Paris, where he built a strong vibrant business under two Kings, an Emperor, and sundry other persons. Unfortunately, when Louis XVII refused to accept James's wife as she was Jewish, James turned to the King and said, "What am I chopped liver?" (only in French), and refused to deal with him any longer. As the French changed Kings, Queens, Emperors and became Republics with incredible regularity, the Rothschild bank in fell out of favour for only a very short time. Royalty and government were the biggest game in town and if what they wanted to do seemed sensible, James took part, and all in a very sophisticated manner which the French appreciated.

The second son Salomon, was sent to Vienna. His personality suited the Viennese because he dotted his i's and crossed his t's, and the Viennese like everything just so. He had the type of sophistication that belongs only to the Viennese. You have to know one to understand it. While handling the financial matters of Maria Theresa and her son Joseph II, he also found the money for Kaiser Ferdinand's Nordbahn (his Northern Railway which he had constructed to connect Vienna with the salt mines in Bochnia near Kraków). Salomon's bank did extremely well.

Third son, Nathan, was sent to England, for which he also had the right sort of personality. He had the quirkiness of the English, while retaining the family's banking prowess. This usually worked out fine and blended in with the way the English tended to do things. Any banker with a mind to strictly follow the rules and never deviate would not cope with England. Nathan opened his bank in Manchester, which was growing into a large mill town. He found his feet working with the mill owners, then he started to deal on the stock exchange, buying and selling gold. At one stage he transferred enough money to pay Wellington's troops (not necessarily the act of a sane dot your i's cross your t's banker, as at that stage no one was actually sure who was going to win). In 1826 he supplied the Bank of England with enough coinage to avert a liquidity problem. He played a huge role in helping Britain in abolishing its involvement with the slave trade by enabling it to buy out the plantation owners.

Things did not go so well for Carl, his brother, in Naples. What with Napoleon trying to sort out Italy and the muddle the Vatican had got itself into, he had his hands full. He was able to stabilise the Vatican to an extent. (They were so delighted with him they even forgot he was Jewish.) However, he decided that trying to run a sensible bank in Italy was like herding cats, so the bank was closed down.

One of the Rothschild major strengths was that they stuck together; something that was drummed into them as children, this was a family business and the family were as one. What they did was nobody else's business. They operated what amounted to a "pony express" that ran the whole time between the banks. As a result, they knew who had won the Battle of Waterloo two days before anyone else. They were made Barons, built themselves big houses, and are still with us.

CHAPTER 45

The Sassoons

The Sassoons, though Jewish, were very different from the Rothschilds. They were Sephardi Jews. (As I mentioned in my introduction, when the Sephardi Jews began to use surnames, they often chose common Christian names - pardon the expression - as their surnames, which meant you could end up with names such as Joseph Joseph or Emanuel Emanuel, though I must admit I have never heard of a Sassoon Sassoon).

The Sassoons were in Bagdad for hundreds of years and were treated liked princes. They handled all the pasha's money and traded with the entire world. They were regarded as Jewish royalty, until along came an unfriendly pasha who, realising just how much money the Sassoons had compared with his own wealth, began to persecute them. David Sassoon made a stand against him, but finally had to flee with his family to India, where he set up an equally successful business with tentacles all over the world. They started opening banks as they realised it was the only way they could lend money to people without putting themselves in a position of having to lend money to someone with immense power who might suddenly realise they could never pay back the debt. After all, though an individual or family could be thrown out of a country, it was much harder to throw out a bank, particularly one that was doing well.

The Sassoons also profited from the opium wars, which were caused when traders buying Chinese goods found the easiest way of paying their accounts was with shipments of opium. This didn't sit well with

China's ruling Qing Dynasty, who didn't feel that having half the population zonked out of their mind was a very good thing; so they went to war, first with Britain, and then with Britain and France. However, in each case, they were defeated by the modern military technology of the European forces

David, along with his son, Abdullah, whose name was later modified to Albert, constructed the West India Docks. Later Albert came to England and became not only the first Sassoon to wear western style clothes, but was a great friend of the Prince of Wale and a member of parliament. With the Sassoons' move to England, they opened trading houses and banks which are still trading today.

At one stage the Shah of Persia came on a state visit. As neither Queen Victoria nor the Prince of Wales could stand him, they dragged in Albert Sassoon, who spoke Persian, to help entertain him. The poor man was really quite ill at the time, but felt that, as a good friend of the Prince of Wales, he had to agree. This upset some of the Jewish community, who believed he shouldn't have anything to do with a ruthless persecutor of their race. Despite being unwell, Albert valiantly stuck by the Shah's side through all the engagements and took over the Empire State Theatre for what was the climax of the Shah's visit; this was basically the first Royal Command Performance. Everyone who was anyone was either performing or in the audience. After the show there was a splendid supper. When the Sassoons' put on a "do", no expense was spared. When it was all over Albert was created the First Baron of Kensington, acknowledging that it had been no easy matter entertaining the Shah and keeping him out of people's hair. As Albert had also helped secure a concession that blocked Russia's designs on Persia, the powers that be felt it was the least they could do.

The Sassoons, like the Rothschilds before them, became part of British society. Siegfried Sassoon, Alfred's son, was one of the great World War I poets. He was named Siegfried not because of any German ancestry - there was none - but because his mother loved Wagner's "The Ring Cycle" (so not everyone thought "Is this never going to end?").

CHAPTER 46

The British East India Company

The British East India Company began when Raleigh captured a huge Portuguese ship stacked to the gunnels with jewels, pearls, gold and all sorts of stuff that the Portugese had been trading with the East. "This trading is obviously profitable", thought Queen Elizabeth I, and immediately granted the East India Company a charter to trade, starting around 1600. There were sundry fights with the Portuguese who finally amalgamated with the Dutch to become a company and issue shares.

At first The British East India Company were not so interested in India or building any sort of empire, they were just traders. It was "Clive of India", as he was known, who pulled the whole thing together. Robert Clive was a soldier who worked for the East India Company and became Commander-in Chief, taking over the trading in large parts of Southern Asia. He became incredibly rich. He was considered far too flashy, but managed to control virtually the whole of India when he overthrew the unpopular heir to the throne of Bengal and also defeated the French. He returned to Britain and joined the Tory party. He annoyed his fellow politicians, as far as I can make out, by being far flamboyant and much too rich, so they put him on trial for corruption. Nothing came of it as it finally occurred to people it was not against the law to be rich or flashy, so he was given The Order of the Bath.

In 1803, someone in the British Government took a look at the British East India Company, only to discover it had a larger army than the British. They decided this was not a good thing and took it over after a rebellion, and this started The British Raj. It also marked the decline of the East India Company, which was up to its ears in sending opium to China, and, as mentioned, the Opium wars that followed.

CHAPTER 47

Odds and Ends

Around the late 1700s came the birth of the gentlemen's club. Two were especially notable: White's was where the Tories gathered to get away from their wives, read, smoke, drink, gamble and generally be convivial. Brooks's, which grew out of two of the members of White's being blackballed so they started their own club, ending up with many of the same members, but this time the majority were Whigs. One of the members was Beau Brummell, at the time when he and the Prince Regent were friends. Both clubs still exist today.

(If you really want to get the feel of life in the Regency period, read Georgette Heyer. Oh, I know, it's a sort of chick lit, but there is no one who captured that era better than she did.)

Then there was Raffles, Thomas Stamford Bingley Raffles. With a name like that you have to be in some way important. He started off as a clerk in the East India Company. He grew in stature and was obviously very good at negotiations, but his main claim to fame was that he acquired Singapore for Great Britain, and now has a lovely hotel named after him, which sends a Rolls Royce to pick guests up from the airport. It also has a "Long Bar" against which many famous people have propped themselves, including Noel Coward and Somerset Maugham. The bar also famous for its Gin Sling. (See what interesting, useless information my mind collects, absolutely nothing to do with wars, acts of parliament, or such, just pieces of trivia, here and there.)

In 1821 Mexico declared its independence from Spain without any appreciable loss of blood. Texas seceded from Mexico and dithered about until 1845 when it joined the U.S.A. New Zealand accepted British rule in 1840.

In Britain, Sir Robert Peel was Prime Minister under William IV and Victoria. He very unwillingly supported the Catholic Emancipation Act, but he did remove the duty on corn, which went some way towards helping the starving Irish. He also reorganized the police force, which is why in cockney slang they are sometimes referred to as Peelers or more often Bobbies.

In 1850, Australia legislated to set up a council in New South Wales. This was the first move towards independence for the penal colony.

CHAPTER 48

The Victorians

It took a while for everyone to realize that the hopes of all Britain rested on Victoria's tiny shoulders. In his rush to produce an heir, her father, Prince Edward, Duke of Kent, married one of the most unpleasant women you could possibly meet, and then had to the good sense to die, horrified he might have to spend any more time with his wife than was absolutely necessary. Victoria's mother, Princess Victoria, disliked England, couldn't speak the language and was a natural born schemer. She couldn't stand Victoria's uncle, King William, who she thought was an oversexed fool.

She collected around her King Leopold of the Belgians and her private secretary. Their plan was to have complete control over the young Victoria. The poor child wasn't allowed a bedroom of her own, she always had to sleep with Mother. As far as she dared, the princess kept her daughter away from any of her father's relatives.

As Victoria herself wrote, she had a very dismal childhood. King William's plan to stay alive until Victoria reached eighteen and therefore not need a regent worked, but only just. When she was summoned from her bedroom and stood there in her nightie to be told William died and she was now queen, the first thing she said was, "Right-ho, I'm going to have my own bedroom."

Young Victoria liked men, especially good-looking men, so she was very lucky the Prime Minister of the time, Lord Melbourne, was extremely good-looking, and gentle with her. Having had to deal with his unruly wife, Caroline, organising a sane woman, who happened to have a crush on him, was a delight. He taught her and protected her as much as possible from her mother and her cohorts. Her mother suddenly realized she was no longer in control and had under-estimated her daughter.

As Salic law decreed only a man was acceptable as the ruler, Victoria could not inherit Hanover, so her highly unpopular uncle, the Duke of Clarence, became King of Hanover. The British people were pleased to get rid of him.

Now that she was queen, the main aim in everyone's life was to get Victoria married off and have her produce an heir. After a lot of huffing and puffing, she decided she would marry Prince Albert of Saxe-Coburg and Gotha, her uncle Leopold's favourite. He was a very serious young man but, unexpectedly, they fell madly in love. Victoria spent the next few years being pregnant, but she was not what you'd call a natural-born mother, and she thought new born babies would be much nicer if they had a little fur like her pet dog. While she was pregnant with her first child, one Edward Oxford took a pot shot at her. He missed but was tried for treason. It was decided he was mad and he was sent to Australia.

Life began to slowly change from the racy Regency period. It became far more serious and everyone discovered it was a good thing to have a sense of morality, which had never been considered terribly important during the late seventeenth and early eighteenth centuries. Now family life was the thing. One went to church regularly, and right was right and wrong was wrong. This was a bit hard on poor Lord Melbourne who was a true Regency character.

The next thing of note that I know about, although not very much, was the Crimean War, which began in 1853 and lasted for over two years. It started with the Christian minorities wanting rights to the Holy Land. Those involved were Britain, France, Prussia, Russia and Sardinia (of all places), with the Ottoman Empire on the other side. They kept trying to make with each other, then one would disagree, and Napoleon II of France wouldn't agree with anyone.

Finally, Russia got tired of "Yes, we're fighting, no we're not", and attacked everyone. It ended up with Russia losing and the Ottoman Empire being greatly weakened.

There are streets all over Britain named after the various battles, but the only battle I know anything about at all is Balaclava, where the charge of the Light Brigade took place. The British sent six hundred cavalry officers into certain death and are incredibly proud of it. Why anyone would be proud of killing off six hundred men for no apparent reason is beyond me. Tennyson wrote a poem about them. There is something in the British psyche, a sort of combination of appearing to be slightly mad to other people but perfectly sane to the British, and the ability to obey orders, bravery, and "What the hell maybe it'll work out". It was the same in The Second World War when young air force men, some no older than nineteen, flew mission after mission, knowing that the likelihood of being shot down was one in four.

It was not only soldiers who served in the Crimean war. There were others, such Florence Nightingale, who virtually trained herself to be a nurse. This predominantly consisted of washing one's hand (you see, she had something there) and keeping things as clean as possible, which of course was a good thing. Because she was friendly with Sidney Herbert, who was secretary for war at the time, he wangled it that she and a bunch of other young women went out to help with the wounded. Nowadays some people claim she and her cohorts were a bit of a nuisance during the war, but she did achieve a great deal, including getting the government to make portable hospitals that could be sent out to the battle-site. She basically learnt on the job as it were, and when she got home she established a Nursing School at St. Thomas's Hospital.

Wars were weird, they still are for that matter, but in the late eighteenth and early nineteenth centuries, the army was run by gentlemen. You could buy yourself a commission and they all thought they should play by gentlemen's rules. Every so often someone was thrown up who actually knew what they were doing, such as Henry V, John Churchill, Napoleon, Nelson, Wellington, Hannibal and Alexander the Great, and possibly a few others that I don't know about, but basically he who won was whoever had the most men and didn't care if those men got killed.

World War I was a prime example of idiocy. It was run by generals who were too old, didn't know anything about modern warfare nor what they should do with the new-fangled weapons they had at their disposal.

English history is littered with characters that do things that tend to make no sense at all and then, later on, everyone looks up to them as great heroes. Gordon of Khartoum is an example. He was a general who had been around at the time. When an uprising broke out in the Sudan he was sent there and made governor-general. He came face to face with a self-styled Mardi, Mohammed Ahsan. Gordon captured Khartoum and sent a message back to England that he would hold the fort for England. He was told not to bother, they didn't want Khartoum, and to come home at once. "No, I will hold Khartoum", was his reply. "Come home and don't be silly." "I will stand and save it for Great Britain." The fact that Great Britain didn't want it, didn't seem to penetrate. Of course, he got himself killed. Now everyone regards him as a great hero, if a little soft in the head.

Back to Victoria, Britain wanted to bring in a bill against homosexuality. When they presented it to Her Majesty, she read it and said, "Well, yes, all right for men, but women don't behave like that. Of course not, I won't have it." There was no moving her from this position. So, homosexual men were picked on but the women were left alone.

Victoria fell in love with Scotland, and having got rid of Uncle Clarence, felt free to spend lots of time there, draping herself and the rest of the family in tartan.

At one point Canada revolted. Robert Nelson declared independence for lower Canada. Lord Melbourne, the then Prime Minister, sent Lord Durham to sort it out. Durham was one of those people who can start a fight in an empty room. He had been part of the government, but Lord Melbourne got sick and tired of the havoc he caused and kicked him out. Even out of government he still made a nuisance of himself, and Melbourne, who liked a peaceful life, was at his wit's end, trying to think of what to do with Durham. When Canada needed attention, he thought, "Brilliant. Durham, go to Canada, sort it out, and stay there for a long, long time". Durham caused major havoc, of course, but when the dust settled, it turned out he hadn't done a bad job of it, and the two parts of Canada were reunited, although not before annoying almost everyone concerned.

Meanwhile, what to do with Prince Albert? He was, in fact, very intelligent and well organized, and would have been useful aiding the government had he been allowed to, but both the government and the queen would not hear of it. Victoria behaved like Miranda Richardson in Black Adder if it was suggested that Alfred had a thought of his own. "Who's queen?" was her tart response. The poor man seemed to spend most of his time tidying up Buckingham Palace and the running there of, which had been a shambles. Then came along the idea of holding the 1851 Festival of Britain. Showing off Britain in all its glory to the world, and who better to arrange it than Prince Albert?

The government was very much an "old boys club". Most of them had known each other their whole lives, attending the same schools and universities. The worst thing they failed to do was look after Ireland. I was ashamed to be English when I read about this. As I said before, it more or less started when William of Orange arrived to take up the throne and gave all his chums bits of Ireland. They mostly lived in England and were absentee landlords, taking large rents from their tenants and leaving them with very little. They managed to get away with this because potatoes were cheap and plentiful, so the Irish managed to subsist for years on a diet made up mainly of potatoes. Then came the four years of potato blight. The British Government was warned over and over again, but their heads were full of Corn Laws and who was allowed to vote. They gave Ireland the vote and considered that to be sufficient. And who'd want to eat potatoes, anyway?

The British public were pretty well blithely unaware of the how dire the Irish situation was until someone wrote a paper after four long years, stating that in the whole of Europe no working-class people were as mistreated as the Irish, and that a million people had died of starvation. It went on to say that thousands of them had migrated to New York, and in time had taken over Tammany Hall and the police force. The British Government was horrified, but the damage was done. Queen Victoria's heart went out to Irish, but too late. That they had let it happen in the first place is a very black mark against them.

Disraeli was another Prime Minister I find interesting. The very fact that he had fights with Gladstone makes him even more so. His father had an argument with his local rabbi, and made the whole family turn Anglican, though I have no idea how much attention he actually paid to religion. When he came to power, the Queen referred to him in her diary as "A ridiculous old man and quite crazy". It was said, though, that in time Victoria came to quite like him - which was rare among her various Prime Ministers - despite the fact that he was so upright, stern, and in all things correct. Most people simply felt they wanted him to just go away and leave them alone.

Another thing I find fascinating about Disraeli was how he dealt with the troubles over the construction of the Suez Canal after Frenchman Ferdinand de Lesseps obtained concessions from Saad Pasha, the Khedive of Egypt. The Egyptians treated their workforce abominably, and then it turned out the Pasha had no money. When Disraeli heard about all these goings on, he went to his friend banker Nathan Rothschild and said, "Can you please lend me four million pounds?" Nathan starred at him and replied, "What on earth for?"

"I want to buy half the Suez Canal."

"Why?"

"It will be very good for the country."

"And do they know about this?"

"Not yet."

"Are you mad?"

"Call it 'Jewish chutzpah'".

"I thought you were an Anglican?"

"Well, when I need chutzpah I'm Jewish".

"On your head be it."

And, of course, it worked out brilliantly. He got the Bill to buy half the canal through parliament, made Britain a top trading nation, and the canal went on making a fortune for Britain for at least the next hundred years.

Gladstone, on the other hand, was the epitome of the Victorian gentleman. He had a family, went to church, and did all the right things. Queen Victoria couldn't stand him. Too much morality clashing with too much morality. He apparently was a great orator. He trained as a barrister. He voted against slavery, though he made sure his father, who had more than two thousand slaves in his Caribbean plantation, got £106,000 in compensation, which in today's money is around AUD$9,000,000.

Gladstone had difficulty finding a wife. He had to ask three women before one finally said yes, which probably goes to show how deadly boring he was. One of his little oddities was that he liked to go out at night to find young prostitutes and either take them to his home (which must have delighted his wife), or go to where they lived, and try to talk them out of their way of life. He also supported the Church of the Penitentiary, which - like Gladstone - spent a lot of time telling prostitutes that God did not approve of them and they really should be doing something else. During that era, the economic situation for unmarried working-class women was, to say the least, difficult. For instance, if one lost her job as a housemaid because the man of the house was sexually harassing her, and the lady of the house blamed her and dismissed her from the home without references (which happened all too frequently), the only likelihood of her getting another job was either in a factory - if she could find such work - or take up the oldest profession. In despair, some of them took to drink, which often made them ill, especially if they got into home-made gin. As the women had so few options, Gladstone and the church spent years lecturing them and getting nowhere.

The British public found his behaviour very strange, but as he didn't appear to be doing any harm or drinking the gin, they decided he was obviously eccentric but harmless. He was around for so long in one way or another that people tended to ignore him. This would seem to me a little difficult over the periods when he was prime minister.

When Prince Albert died of typhoid in 1861, Victoria went into deep mourning, and it took extreme pressure to get her to attend to any of her royal duties. (When her eldest son, the Prince of Wales, also got typhoid - although he pulled through - the Queen put it down to him having an affair with an actress; of course, there had been no such thought about the now-saintly Prince Albert.) The grief-stricken Victoria continued to be extremely difficult to deal with until she discovered Mr. Brown, a Ghillie on her Scottish estate, and things brightened up. He took over and bossed her about in a kindly sort of way, and they became inseparable, much to the horror of all around. When he died, she announced she was going to write a book about her "Dear Mr. Brown". Everyone took a step back and said, "Oh, no, no, no...not a good idea". As the public already felt that she was having an affair with him - which made her very unpopular - a book of adoration about Mr. Brown would be the last straw. She was, in fact, an extremely good writer and kept a diary all her life and would have made an excellent journalist.

Her eldest daughter, Vickie, married Wilhelm I of Germany, who also happened to be an emperor, making Vickie an empress. This didn't go down at all well with the Queen, Empresses out rank Queens, five-to-one

"I want to be an Empress too."

The powers-that-be looked around and decided India needed an empress. So, Queen Victoria became the Empress of India, and was also given the Koh-I-Noor (one of the largest cut diamonds in the world and now part of the Crown Jewels).

In the middle of all this we have the Boer War, in Africa, which I really don't understand. I know it had something to do with the British wanting to take over the land settled by Dutch farmers, known as the Boers, because they found diamonds (always a big incentive to take over land). In the end the British won.

One time, Victoria was very ill with some sort of boil, which Dr. Lister lanced and used his antiseptic for the first time. I don't think the Queen was aware she was being used as a guinea pig. However, it did popularise the use of antiseptics and possibly the washing of hands. The way some doctors treated people before this, it seems amazing anyone ever lived through any sort of operation.

Victoria was still deeply unpopular with the public until she was shot at by an enraged poet. (This was, in fact, the eighth attempt to assassinate her!) Robert Maclean had apparently submitted a poem to her and she had rejected it somewhat curtly, hence his rather overstated response.

Her popularity immediately soared. As she said, "It's really quite worth being shot at to gain such a nice result".

The Queen didn't like not having a man about the place. She looked around and noticed an Indian servant who took her fancy. Everyone was horrified, another Mr. Brown, but more so. She, however, insisted that he was her "munshi", which was some sort of teacher, and nothing could dislodge her from him. Even when it was discovered he was a complete fake and liar, the Queen didn't care. She and took him everywhere with her, and he taught her Urdu and stayed by her side until her death.

For her diamond jubilee in 1897, everything had to be changed because of her grandson Wilhelm II, no one could stand him as he was always unpleasant and often given to throwing wild threats around. They invited only heads of states of all the self-governing dominions and no foreign heads of state. It was the only way to avoid asking Wilhelm, because no one ever knew how he would behave.

CHAPTER 49

American Civil War

While all the various goings on in Europe were happening, America was stirring. The North had for some time been against slavery, and, with the coming of the Industrial Revolution, now had money. The South couldn't imagine how it would manage without its slaves. My knowledge of the American Civil War is very limited and is almost entirely reliant on "Gone with the Wind". However, I do know that when Lincoln became President this immediately sent the south into a frenzy and they attacked Fort Sumter. The leader of the southern forces was Robert E. Lee.

The Union leader was General Ulysses Grant. The South appeared to be winning the war at first, but then the Union forces began to infiltrate the South, destroying most of its infrastructure. Then came the battle of Gettysburg, which the Union finally won and Lincoln gave his famous speech, "Four score and seven years ago...". Five days after the surrender, Lincoln was shot by John Wilkes Booth while attending the theatre. Someone asked, "Why did he do it?"

The answer, "He's an actor".

It was a very bloody war and thousands were killed on both sides. Slavery was abolished and it took the South a very long time to recover from what was virtually a scorched earth policy that the Union army had inflicted upon it.

General Custer fought at the Battle of Gettysburg, where he commanded the Michigan Cavalry Brigade, and, despite being outnumbered, defeated the southerners. He eventually met his match, however, in 1876 at the Battle of Little Big Horn in which Sitting Bull flattened him and his whole regiment.

By the end of the nineteenth century, they had assassinated three presidents, and four more had died in office. There had been two presidents called "Adams" (in the next century there'd another two called "Roosevelt"). And during all this, they were slowly on their way to becoming a top nation and doing it in a "Goodness, gracious me, shucks, how did this happen?" sort of way.

Things did not become equal in America, although blacks were not considered slaves any longer, they were - and often still are - treated very badly. I remember a girlfriend of mine telling me how she was in Los Vegas with Sammy Davis and his wife Altorvise. They were walking down the main street and Sammy said, "You know five years ago this wouldn't have been allowed."

"What?", she asked, puzzled.

"A black man walking down the street alongside a white woman."

That was in the early 70s, but even today there is still a great deal of inequality in the USA.

(Apart from the major cities, I think America is quite isolationist. I find most Americans are quite loveable, but it took them years to realise Australia was not in the Alps. It was only when "Crocodile Dundee" came out that they realised where it actually was, and greeted every Australian they met with "Put another shrimp on the barbie".)

CHAPTER 50

The Suffragettes

Towards the end of the 1800's women were beginning to get a proper education. There had always been clever, intelligent females around, but now they were getting into universities, but not without great difficulty. People like Emmeline Pankhurst popped up with political aspirations. I don't know that she actually wanted to get into parliament, she just wanted women to have the vote. In the early part of the century it had been hard enough to for men to get men the vote, so her "Women's Social and Political Union" didn't go down at all well with the males in power. Or most men, in fact.

"We've only just got the Irish sorted out. I knew we shouldn't have done that. Now look what's happened. Women want to vote. What on earth for? Haven't they got enough to do, finding a husband, having babies, cooking, knitting, tatting or whatever it's called? They should be happy giving dinner parties."

Men really didn't understand that women had been involved in politics for hundreds of years, as it was often the women behind powerful men who were pulling the strings. A few men conceded that there might be some bright ones around, but, overall, the basic male attitude was that as most women didn't own anything (because everything a wife possessed belonged to her husband), why should they get to vote?

The Women's Social and Political Union went into full action mode. At first the men just found them annoying. They marched with banners, demanding to vote. They chained themselves to railings. Those few with money refused to pay tax. (That had worked for the Americans.) Someone had the bright idea of putting them in jail. Detained, they went on hunger strikes. Not good, so they were force-fed; really bad. Those in charge were beginning to realise this was turning into a P.R. disaster. Then Evelyn Wilding Dawson went to the Derby and threw herself under the King's horse, getting killed in the process. Major horror all around. But this only proved to the powers in charge that women were completely emotionally unstable: "And they think they should get to vote?".

Meanwhile, the managers of stores like Liberty and Selfridges saw a great marketing opportunity. They produced ribbons and rosettes and various other things in the colours of the WSPU. Mappin and Web produced brooches for the suffragettes to wear.

The main problem for the WSPU was that most women were not terribly interested in politics and voting. Most of them had virtually no education, and as long as they could work as maids or shop girls or run a household as a dutiful wife that was all that was required of them. The men should have settled down and realised that as voting in Britain was not compulsory, then, even if they got the right to vote, most women would have either not bothered or voted as their husbands directed them. Only a small handful of women actually wanted it.

However, that handful made enough of a nuisance of themselves until, finally, in 1918 women over 30 were allowed to vote, and in 1928 all women got the right. And, men discovered, surprisingly, that nothing dreadful happened. The world stayed on it's axis.

CHAPTER 51

The Gold Rush

It was the start of second half of the nineteenth century and all of a sudden everyone was chasing gold. It was discovered in California and Alaska and Australia, where it was all over the place, but the main sources were around Ballarat and Bendigo, in central Victoria.

People flocked from all over the world to get rich quick. It must have been incredibly difficult to get to the various places as there were no railways, but the finding of gold soon made small towns into large rich ones. Melbourne was built on the money from the goldfields of Ballarat and Bendigo. It became an extremely rich city with very imposing buildings.

The first Australian parliament was opened in Melbourne in 1901 at the Royal Exhibition Building (at that time the only building large enough to fit all the invited guests), but thereafter parliament was located in the Victorian Parliament House. In 1927, they moved the location of parliament to the national capital city of Canberra. I know more about Australia because even though I was born and raised in England, I live in Australia now and have done so for many years.

I think it very likely that everywhere there were gold rushes, the people who became the richest were the ones who didn't dig for gold but who opened shops to supply the miners with whatever they needed.

In 1854 the miners in Ballarat rebelled against very high taxes and miners' licences. They built themselves a stockade and produced their own flag. It was blue with a white cross and they called it "The Eureka Flag".

The British Government took a very dim view of a bunch of miners demanding their rights, and sent in the British troops. Although Victoria was a state of Australia, it was still under the control of Britain. Twenty seven miners were killed on sight but about sixty others died from their injuries. Peter Lalor, who had been elected head of the striking miners was shot in the left arm, which had to be amputated. The Government troops went in hard, but the second-in-command, Captain Charles Paisley, was horrified at the carnage and stopped them bayoneting a group of miners. John King, a trooper, took down the Eureka flag.

Back in Melbourne, the British Government was facing a PR crisis. The new state of Victoria was not about to let its citizens be slaughtered for what they saw as a perfect right to revolt against high licences and taxes. Attempts to get some of the local male population to join the Government troops got nowhere. There was a great to-do and the Government had to admit maybe it had gone too far. Nevertheless, it was determined to charge the miners and put them in jail. Something like thirteen miners were brought to trial. It took the jury half an hour to decide they were not guilty, and the government was left with egg on its face.

Peter Lalor later became a parliamentarian, and Charles Paisley was mentioned in dispatches to Britain, possibly as being the only sane person there.

CHAPTER 52

Emperor Franz Joseph of Austria

The Austrian royal family could only marry people from a reigning house, such as the Bavarian royal family, and so for generations these two royal families kept intermarrying and producing children. It's amazing that weren't all crackers - some of them were.

Franz Joseph was not actually in line to take over the throne. His uncle the Emperor Ferdinand, who was supposed to inherit the throne, was - to say the least - "one sandwich short of a picnic", and the powers that be decided between themselves that he was not mentally stable enough to take the throne. It would have to be someone else.

Franz Joseph's mother, Sophia of Bavaria had groomed her son Franz Joseph - she always referred to him as "Franzi" - for the position from an early age. Her husband, the Archduke Karl, didn't seem to be interested in the throne, nor anything in particular, so (with a little urging from Sophia) he abdicated his right to be emperor, leaving the way clear for his son, Franz Joseph.

At the age of thirteen, Franz, in preparation to becoming Kaiser, joined the colonial army, as later did both his brothers. He was put under the command of Field Marshal Radetzky (in whose honour the famous march by Strauss Snr. was named). Franz Joseph served on the Italian front and acquitted himself well for a thirteen-year-old. The army life set him up to become very organised (a good thing if you're going to rule a country). From the time he joined the army he always wore military uniform, which turned out to be a very fortuitous. When one of his officers, Count Maximillian Karl O'Donnell (a very Irish name for an Austrian!), tried to cut his throat, the knife hit the stiff army collar, saving his life. No particular reason seems to have been given as to why he wanted to kill Franz Joseph; after the trial O'Donnell was hanged.

Ferdinand was persuaded to sign an agreement to stand down, and Franz Joseph was created emperor in 1848. Great things were expected of the young and vibrant new emperor.

Early in Franz Joseph's reign, the Royal Family had to flee Vienna to Innsbruck. The Hungarians were revolting, as usual. So, a deal was made with the Russians that they would keep Hungary under control (they seemed to cope with the nature of the Hungarians better than the Austrians did), and Austria would stop Prussia from creating a new German federation. In the end, however, to keep the peace, the Hungarians were made part of the Austro-Hungarian Empire.

Franz Joseph fell madly in love in love with Duchess Elizabeth of, naturally, Bavaria. She was known as 'Sissi", was very beautiful, but, unfortunately, not terribly interested in Franz Joseph. Even so they married and managed to have four children, Archduchess Sophie, Gisela, Marie Valerie, and Crown Prince Rudolf.

Sissi was a fairly wild soul. She took up the Hungarian cause and spent more and more of her time there riding horses, leave Franz Joseph lonely in Vienna. He spent his time shooting wild animals, while weaving between the various states under his care, who were either revolting or facing other countries trying to take over Austria. Meanwhile, he found himself a lady friend, an actress called Katharina Schratt, who stayed around for the rest of his life. One book claims their relationship was purely platonic. Who knows? Anyway, they used to meet at his hunting lodge, Mayerling, in a place call Bad Ischl. (This has been preserved as a tourist attraction. I went to visit it, and I have never seen so many heads of dead animals in my life. It was horrible. I know that aristocrats like to spend a lot of their time having shooting parties, but couldn't they kill things with a little less gusto?)

Franz Joseph's younger brother, Maximillian, was made Emperor of Mexico in 1864. At that time, Europe had control of Mexico, which was in need of an emperor. The Europeans were so used to picking any available person and popping him into the job of king or emperor when needed that they gave no thought to the fact that the Mexicans, having been invaded by the Spanish years ago, might not have the temperament to have a Prussian-type Emperor suddenly land on their doorstep. Poor Maximillian; it wasn't his fault as he was a very capable man in his own field. Unfortunately, that field wasn't dealing with the fiery Mexicans. He became Emperor in 1863, but was executed by the restored Republican government three years later. The moral there would surely be that it's better to ask people first if they want something before foisting on them whatever you think they ought to have.

Serbia was one of the most difficult places to control, as everybody wanted to own it. I wondered what's so interesting about Serbia, and discovered that, as well as being practically in the very middle of eastern Europe, it was the gateway to the Black Sea and then onto the Mediterranean; therefore, everyone wanted Serbia. The Ottoman Empire was beginning to crumble by this stage after hundreds of years, and various countries were coming up for grabs and everyone wanted what they could grab. Russia wanted Bosnia-Herzegovina, and Prussia also thought it would be nice to have it. So, they all batted back and forth in the sort of Eastern European tussle that had been going on for years, but this time without the strength of the Turks' Ottoman Empire, who had previously usually won. This time Austria won, and hung on to Serbia.

For years Prussia had been going on about uniting Germany, and waged several wars to make it so. Finally, there was the Franko-Prussia war in 1870 when they got their own way, and Kaiser Wilhelm I became Emperor of all those little unpronounceable states that had been cluttering up most of Europe for years. In 1871 they all became Germany, but it was really Prussia.

Wilhelm I seemed quite a nice man and he married Queen Victoria's daughter, Vicki. Their son Wilhelm II, however, was a major nightmare. It may not have been his fault entirely. He was born with one arm shorter than the other and his doctors, in their wisdom, felt if they pulled hard enough on the shorter arm, it would somehow grow to proper length. This must have been agony for the child, and didn't seem to make any appreciable difference to the arm, but I'm sure it went well on the way to making Wilhelm II a raging neurotic and impossible to deal with. He wanted desperately to be popular, but was one of those people who have no idea how to go about getting people to like him. He tried gushing all over them until they felt revolted and pushed him away, and when they did, he stamped his foot and became autocratic to an impossible degree. People tended to cross the road when they saw him coming, as it were. What made him impossible to ignore was that he was related in one way or another to half the crown heads of Europe. His mother was Queen Victoria's daughter, his uncle, Edward VII, was married to a Danish princess, who's sister was Tsar Nicholas II's mother, and they all spent their summer holidays in Denmark, except Wilhelm, who didn't get an invitation.

From about 1867 there was relative peace. Franz Joseph decided to deal with the Hungarian situation by making them sort of co-members of the Austrian Empire; from then on it was the Austro-Hungarian Empire which shut most of the troublemakers up for a while, though Bosnia-Herzegovina was still being difficult. It had been under the control of the Turks as part of the Ottoman Empire and was therefore Islamic. As the Turks were slowly losing their Ottoman Empire, the new Austro-Hungarian Empire took most of it over.

Franz Joseph's son, Rudolph, and the heir to the throne, whose rather unstable temperament may well have been the result of a surfeit of the royal Austrian/Bavarian marriages, was found dead in his shooting lodge at Mayerling, with his companion Baroness Marie Vetsers. It was called a murder-suicide. I don't think that was true at all. Though Rudolph was certainly a bit of a flake, I think they were both murdered. It was true he'd been wandering around for several years saying, "Wouldn't it be romantic to kill yourself and your lover?" (When he brought up the subject with his lady friend at the time, she roared with laughter, told him not to be so silly and never saw him again.) Finally, he found himself a rather naive seventeen-year-old, who became caught up in the romance of it all and wrote copious amounts about it in her diary.

Everyone went into shock when their bodies were found. At first it was said he'd been poisoned, which was patently rubbish as they had both clearly been shot and there was blood everywhere. Then they said he did it because he had gonorrhoea and was taking morphine for it, which was affecting his eyes. (To start with, if people killed themselves because of gonorrhoea, half the aristocracy of the world at that period would been dead too. Anyway, the treatment for gonorrhoea was not morphine, which apparently makes you sleepy. The treatment was mercury, which could poison you if you took too much, but didn't affect the eyes.) In my opinion, people who spend several years walking around telling other people they are thinking of killing themselves are very unlikely to actually do it. They say it more for effect than fact.

Rudolph was a Mason, which upset the Catholic church no end, so someone came up with the idea that the Masons killed both of them. I don't think Masons go around killing each other. I don't know much about them (what I do know is they wear little aprons, have funny hand shakes, and see that their brethren get good jobs), but they seem relatively harmless, and I doubt they would knock off a prince, who was one of them and heir to the throne of Austria. Also, like his mother, he was very pro-Hungarian. Hungarians, no matter whatever was done for them, were never the easiest people to deal with, and were quite likely to cause mayhem at the drop of a hat, even though they were now part of the Austro-Hungarian Empire. Also Rudolph had been foolish enough to say "Let's give Bosnia back to the Turks, after all they are Muslim", which upset everyone. Emperor Joseph II's secret police, who were still keeping things in order and monitoring what the people did and said, would not have been at all pleased at the things Rudolph was doing and saying. They wanted stability for Austria and didn't regard Rudolph as the sort of person who should inherit the throne. He'd been going on and on about wanting death for ages, and I believe they gave it to him.

On the morning in 1898 an Italian called Luigi Lucherri had gone out looking for someone to assassinate, rather like someone going out for a coffee. He had planned on it being the Duke of Orleans, but the duke had left town. So, Sissie being available, this lunatic stabbed her to death. Franz Joseph was never the same afterwards.

CHAPTER 53

Edward VII

When Edward the VII eventually succeeded to the British throne in 1901, he was a middle-aged man, who was known as "the first gentleman of Europe". He had affairs with at least half the now British aristocracy's grandmothers and great grandmothers, plus a number of other women. However, he was a great diplomat and if he had been alive I doubt the first World War would ever had happened.

It certainly wouldn't have had Queen Victoria been around. "What does Willie think he's doing? And tell him to stop it." She considered him to be an autocratic idiot, even so he loved her dearly and she died in his arms.

Sadly, for Edward, after too much good living and having nothing much to do for most of his life, he died in 1910, aged 68.

His son George became king, something no one was expecting, as he had an older brother Albert, who suddenly died of pneumonia. George had had no training in kingship. He had spent his time in the royal navy with no real education in how to be the next king of Great Britain.

CHAPTER 54

The lead up to, and aftermath, of World War I

The Austrian were having trouble with the Serbs and the Bosnia-Herzegovina. The problem was that everyone wanted to have access to the Black Sea, and it had become Austria's job, with the disintegration of the Turk's Ottoman Empire - which had formally controlled it - to see things were under control.

Franz Joseph's younger brother had died of typhoid in 1896, so now, with Rudolph gone, the next in line to the Austrian Throne was Franz Joseph's nephew, Franz Ferdinand. Franz fell in love with Sophie Chotek, or, to give her full and very cumbersome title, Countess Sophie Chotek von Chotkow und Wognin.

The bad news was that to marry into the royal house of Habsburg one had to come from a reigning, or formally reigning, dynasty and there didn't appear to be any Bavarians around. The good news was that, in a roundabout sort of way, Sophie was related to practically everyone of any standing, and as Franz Ferdinand wouldn't give her up, permission was given for the wedding to go ahead. None of Franz Ferdinand's family attended and there were only a few there from Sophie's side. But I don't expect it worried the happy couple.

After the ceremony, the two of them continued travelling around the world. They had three children Duchess Sophia of Hohenberg, Duke

Maximilian of Hohenberg and Prince Ernest of Hohenberg. The couple were in Sarajevo on 28th June 1914 when a nineteen-year-old man, a member of "Young Bosnia", shot both of them. Austria retaliated by attacking Serbia, I have no idea why. (One would have thought if one is attacked by a Bosnian that one retaliates against the Bosnians.)

You must remember that although Serbia was a sovereign nation, it was still attached to Russia, which then attacked Austria, and that's how it should have remained, one of the middle-European wars that had been going on for centuries. However, no one wanted a full-blown war against Russia. After all, Russia was very large, and perhaps one would not be able to go home for the winter - look what happened to Napoleon.

England was tottering on the verge of helping Russia, but then in comes Wilhelm II, who had nothing to do with it at all, and attacks Belgium, who had nothing to do with anything. "I'll show them" thought Wilhelm, "not inviting me to their summer holidays".

Belgium really had nothing to do with the European wars. Then Wilhelm, being Wilhelm, started shouting at Russia, and it was on for young and old. Britain and France came out for Russia. It must have come as a big surprise to the English not to be fighting the French, whom they'd been fighting for years, and now instead attacking the Germans, whom most of the Royal Family were related to.

Japan joined in on Russia's side. The Turks tried to stay out of it as their empire was falling to bits anyway, but the Russians made it too difficult, so they sided with Austria. Spain and Portugal did stay out of it, as did the Swiss - no one wanted to fight with them, they were the guardians of everyone's money. Sweden also stayed out of it, mainly because they were apparently supplying both sides with the steel they needed.

The real lunacy started with Gallipoli, which Churchill thought was a good idea, but no one else did. The whole thing was a complete mess from the start, with everyone fighting a twentieth century war in the nineteenth century fashion.

Gallipoli was a bloodletting for the Australian troops. Thousands were killed on both sides, the whole operation resulted in 26,111 Australian casualties, including 8,141 deaths. Eventually it occurred to someone in command that they really weren't going to get anywhere, no matter how many troops they threw into the mix.

On the Western Front they were fighting trench warfare. This actually made me think how sensible they were in the Middle Ages when everyone went home for the winter. The troops that stayed either froze to death or got sucked under by the mud. No one was winning or losing, just dying.

This went on until 1917, when America ruffled itself up. Most of Europe had sort of ignored it as being young, brash and unsophisticated. The Americans had no interest in getting into a war that they considered a purely European catastrophe. They did, however, help with machinery and money, but stayed on the sidelines. But then the Germans sunk the Lusitania, and feelings began to change. After firmly sitting on the fence watching what appeared to be a never-ending trench war, they roused themselves and said, "Oh, for God's sake someone's got to do something about this damned war or it'll go on forever." Clearly it was very bad for business; they had all that cotton and tobacco with no one to sell it to. So, they went in, guns blazing.

The same year, General John Monash was given a free hand by those in command. Monash was not only a soldier but also an architect, an engineer, and a very precise and organised person. He looked at what was going on and thought. "We're doing this all wrong, just sitting in trenches taking pot-shots at one another is useless; the troops need air support and tanks to follow up the first charge." Keith Murdoch an Australian reporter, took it into his head to persuade the Australian Prime Minister, Billy Hughes, that this was all wrong, and the fact Monash was a Jew was not a good thing, but all the generals at the front were behind Monash, as was King George V, so they did it his way.

The Australian's had a great win at Villers Bretonneux (where they repeatedly charged at the enemy until they took the town).

Meanwhile, Lawrence of Arabia, with British blessing, managed to round up most of the Arab tribes to fight on the British side.

For the first time the Germans were terrified at the power the allies actually had and the way they were using it. It suddenly occurred to them perhaps they weren't going to win, especially now the Americans were there in full force.

It didn't take the Americans long, with the aid of the allied powers now out of their trenches, to clean up the whole thing. The armistice declaring the end of hostilities was signed on 11th November, 1918. The peace treaty that followed was signed at Versailles on the 28th June, 1919. Four Empires lost their thrones: the Habsburgs, the Ottoman, the Romanovs, and Hohenlohe (the collective name for all the various Germanic countries such as Bavaria, Prussia, and Germany itself). The treaty was devastating to the Germans. The war also undid all the good things Napoleon had managed to achieve, and the collapse of the Ottoman Empire left lots of land up for grabs.

Once the war was over, Lawrence of Arabia continued to have fun dressing up and aiding and abetting the British. Emir Faisal, who had also aided the British during the war, now wanted something in return. The Arab leader wanted a country for each of his sons; the British blithely cut up parts of the middle east into Trans-Jordan and Iraq, and the rest became Palestine as we know it, which the British held a 25 year mandate over. It was never actually a country but blocks of land, owned by Arabs and Jews.

Emir Faisal brought out a statement: "We Arabs look with the deepest sympathy on the Zionist movement. Our deputation here in Paris is fully acquainted with the proposals submitted yesterday by the Zionist Organisation to the peace conference, and we regard them as moderate and proper. We will do our best, insofar as we are concerned, to help them through; we will wish the Jews a most hearty welcome home…

I look forward, and my people with me look forward, to a future in which we will help you and you will help us, so that the countries in which we are mutually interested may once again take their places in the community of the civilised peoples of the world." My grandson on reading this a hundred years later said, "Yeah, really? Like that's gonna happen any time soon."

CHAPTER 55

Russia

Before World War I ever started the Russians were getting sick and tired of the autocratic way in which they were governed. In the mid 1800's Karl Marx, who was German, had written "Das Kapital", which damned the exploitation of labour.

Made stateless because of his writings, Marx found his way to London, where he and Friedrich Engels, another German, got together and in 1842 wrote the Communist Manifesto.

When Nicholas II came to the Russian throne he was not only weak but he had a wife who was stupid and bossy, too. She kept pushing him into being more and more autocratic, whereas he should have tried to come to some sort of meeting of minds with his government, such as it was. He would stamp his foot and say something like the well-worn "I'm here by divine right!", which was really quite amusing, because, as I've said before, the Romanovs were voted in by committee (no one who is sane imagines a committee has divine rights to do anything). People such and Lenin and Trotsky had been mulling all this over for quite a while.

Nicholas's son had haemophilia, which for some reason, had to be kept a secret. The tsarina fell in with Rasputin who she believed was some sort of holy man. Everyone else loathed and detested him, but she wouldn't have a word said against him. At one stage it was as though he was running the Russian campaign. Some generals conspired to get rid of him, but it proved incredibly difficult. They tried, to no avail, to poison him, stab him, and shoot him, but he finally died when they drowned him.

The October Revolution in 1917 brought Lenin to power and the Soviet Union Communist Party arrived on the scene. They dethroned the tsar and his family and offered to let the British take them, but the Romanov's didn't have a particularly good name with the public, who saw Nicholas as a tyrant, and the British government was frightened of socialism, thus leaving the whole Russian family to be massacred, and White Russians to flee in all directions.

I'm not going to go into Communism, because I don't understand it. What in theory should work, turns out to be a nightmare in reality.

Most Russian were terrified. Thousands of people were killed or dispossessed as they ran away, only to spend the rest of their lives looking over their shoulder, frightened they would be captured and sent to Siberia.

CHAPTER 56

More about the Jews

Before the first world war there had been much talk about the Jews deserving to have their own state and at that point in time, a document know as the "Balfour Declaration" was issued that said: "His Majesty's government view with favour the establishment in Palestine of a national home for the Jewish people and will use their best endeavours to facilitate the achievement of this objective, it being clearly understood that nothing shall be done which may prejudice the civil and religious rights of the existing non-Jewish communities in Palestine, or the rights and political status enjoyed by Jews in any other country."

There were pogroms in Russia, Germany and Poland, and Jews began to drift into Palestine, where they bought land from various Arab absentee landlords. There had always been a few Jews living in Palestine and they managed to live quietly alongside the Arabs. Many of the Arabs they bought land from had no interest in actually living in Palestine and lived in places like Egypt, and were quite happy to get rid of their land in Palestine, which was really not much more than sand dunes and swamps. The attitude seemed to be, if the Jews were silly enough to pay good money for barren land, which for hundreds of years had been of no use to anyone, then let them have it; the Arab owners had no intention of living there.

The Jews however imported trees which soaked up the water and the land became arable. They built schools and hospitals, and many of them lived in agricultural communities, but when they began talking about wanting to form their own state, the Arabs became agitated, and both sides began taking pot-shots at one another.

The Arabs in other countries didn't take it seriously, how could a bunch of farmers take over? The British had a mandate for twenty-five years over Palestine, but when they moved out all hell broke loose. The war of Jewish Independence started in 1947. But that is all for another time, suffice to say the Jews won, but are still fighting about it to this day.

CHAPTER 57

The 1920's, 1930s, and 1940s

One of the first things that happened as the war came to an end was an outbreak of Spanish Flu. It was made far worse because of the movement of people everywhere. By the end of the epidemic it had killed about one third of the world's population, more people than the entire First World War.

Then we had the twenties when everyone went slightly mad. The first thing the American's did was to ban booze. This bright idea absolutely confounds me. It gave a wonderful opening for the mafia, which started in Sicily in the 1800s but was only a minor nuisance in America until prohibition. They stuck their heads up over the parapet, sniffed, looked at each other and someone said, "I smell money." The gang bosses set to work to provide a much-needed product. They were making money big time and nobody seemed able to stop them.

The FBI finally got Al Capone, one of the chief gang bosses on tax avoidance. It also provided the film industry of the thirties and forties with marvellous roles for people such as James Cagney and Edward G. Robinson who made terrific gangsters, and it gave Elliot Ness something to do trying to put the real ones away.

The twenties were full of jazz, short skirts and wild dances. Fashion dictated that women with large breasts should bind them up to appear perfectly flat. Very odd.

Tired of dancing and drinking illicitly, people started buying shares, and the higher the shares went, the more people went into debt to buy more of them. Then came the day of reckoning when they found that they had no money to actually pay for what they'd bought, and what they'd bought wasn't going to make them any money. It is said we are supposed to learn by what happened in history, but of course we don't. No one remembered what happened with the tulips or the South Sea Bubble. In October 1929, the market crashed. Panicked people jumped out of windows, and the world went into deep economic depression. (There's something about October. If there is going to be some sort of disaster, it's more or less certain to happen in October. I have no idea why.) Anyway, the whole world went into recession. No one seemed to know what to do. US President Roosevelt came up with something known as The New Deal, which I gather was a series of work projects and financial reforms. I don't know exactly how it worked, but it did seem to cheer people up a bit.

And then there was Hitler, giving the people something to do by busily arming Germany. Why anyone was surprised that he started the Second World War is beyond me. Everyone sat around during the thirties saying, "Isn't in nice Hitler is giving the Germans something to do? Opening factories and keeping the people busy. And teaching all the youngsters to march. Very organised." What he kept them busy doing seemed to escape them entirely. All the while he had them building tanks, aircraft, and all manner of other warlike paraphernalia. Everyone was so terrified of Communism that most people tended to look upon Hitler's brand of socialism as relatively harmless. He was actually Austrian, not German and he was a megalomaniac who not only put Germany to work to arm themselves for another war, he also trained young people to join the Third Reich, which promoted the idea that the Nazis were the successor of the medieval and early modern Holy Roman Empire (in other words, in power by "Divine right").

Everyone sat blithely by watching this and telling each other how charming he was. My knowledge of the German language is counting up to ten, but listening to some of his speeches where he rants and raves, "charming" would not be the word that comes to mind; I would have thought someone surely should have noticed the man was out of his mind. Apparently, no one voiced concern, at least not in public. The only person who seemed to be aware of this was Churchill, who happened to be writing a book about his ancestor John Churchill, the Duke of Marlborough and noticed the similarities between what Hitler was doing and what Louis IV did in France in the seventeenth century.

No one took any notice of Churchill; he had bungled Gallipoli and was very much out of favour. The barking-mad Hitler wanted Germany to be a pure Aryan race, so he decided all Jews, gypsies and homosexuals had got to go. He rounded them up and sent them to concentration camps. Outsiders heard whispers, but honestly didn't take it too seriously. After all, the Jews made money, which annoyed people without it, gypsies were mostly thieves, and homosexuals were disgusting, so no one worried too much if they were put in prisoner of war camps, which they imagined was all the concentration camps were. It was only when the Americans started liberating them at the end of the war that the full horror was discovered. US General Eisenhower directed his men to take as many photos as possible in case anyone at a later date tried to deny it ever happened. Even today there is still a lunatic element, running around denying the Holocaust ever happened.

What Hitler was doing made no sense at all. He thought the Jews made a perfect scapegoat, why? They had money, but they were a quiet, peaceful people. Maybe people felt jealous because they were good with money, but Jews never got on their high-horse and said, "Everyone must be Jewish" (except for some strange European king, who may or may not have existed, who suddenly turned around and told his whole country they must be Jewish - and look how that turned out when Ferdinand and Isabella wanted everyone to be Catholic - but I'm not sure it actually happened. Still, Arthur Koestler thought enough about it to write a book called "The Thirteenth Tribe").

The Jews wanted their own country and when the British mandate ended in 1948, the Jews declared the State of Israel to exist. My ex-husband was eighteen and in Palestine at the time, and fought in the Israeli War of Independence.

Meanwhile, prior to all that, the British had their own problem with the Duke and Duchess of Windsor. I'm no fan of hers. She had her claws into David, who would become Edward VII when he became king (changing your name when you become king is a very British thing to do). At first, she probably thought, "Wouldn't it be fun to be Queen of Britain?", then she discovered the British people didn't think having her as queen would be fun at all, and, anyway, it wouldn't be allowed because she was a divorcee. She realised she had attached herself to a very weak man who refused to give her up and gave up his country instead. She could do nothing but spend of the rest of her life being loathed and detested by the British public and most of the Royal Family.

As soon as you open your mouth most people in Britain know where you come from and what school you went to. If you want to belong to the upper crust there are thousands of little pitfalls. For instance, you don't say "pardon?", you say "what?". (But whoever said the British upper class were polite? "Pardon?" is considered very middle class; on the other hand, the middle class think it's rude to say "What?".) You mustn't handle your knife as though it's a pen, a serviette is a napkin, you must never cut a bread roll but break it with your hands, and a toilet is a lavatory, and on and on. By the way, if confronted with a formal dinner with it's confusing amount of cutlery, start from the outside and move in. In the 1960 Nancy Mitford and others wrote "Nobless Oblige: An Enquiry into the Identifiable Characteristics of the English Upper Class". This explains the whole thing perfectly.

Meanwhile, back to the Windsor's, who were a nightmare on wheels. Edward (having resigned as king, was now the Duke of Windsor) he was stripped of all his royal titles and inheritances. Although the now King George did grant him, I think, ten thousand pounds a year to live on. Adding to the public's intense dislike of them was the fact that they were both quite pro-Hitler. England had no further use for them, and they were no longer welcome there. So, they wandered about Europe playing king and queen of the Euro-Trash and being supported by a number of rich friends. They finally settled in France. Long after the war a friend of mine wrote a romantic musical about the Duke and Duchess of Windsor, got himself a record deal and then decided to stage it in London. I told him, "For God's sake, don't. Everyone in England hates her. Put it on in New York, it's got a chance there." Sadly, he didn't listen and it didn't do well, though actually it was quite good.

Hitler, with all the nice new weapons he'd been amassing, started invading countries. Although at first the British did nothing except say stupid things like, "Peace in our time", which was patently absurd, then he attacked Poland, which was too much for both Britain and France. France crumbled very quickly. (The then-Duke of Norfolk - no, I haven't forgotten him - was a Major and briefly in the Battle Of France, but was sent home sick, which sounds rather more like school than war!). Russia started by being on the Germans' side, then decided they really didn't like Germany and changed sides. Japan thought it would rather like to take over the Far East and sided with Germany. Norway was taken over by the Germans, but Spain and Portugal managed to remain neutral, as did Switzerland, which was just as well because no one wanted their money interfered with. Sweden also was apparently neutral, and providing yet again materials for the war - for both sides.

Back to the exiled Windsors - what to do about them? For all his weakness Edward was British to the core and wanted to help. His wife was still a staunch Nazi, which seemed to have escaped her husband's notice. The general feeling was that if Hitler won, he would make the Windsor's puppet King and Queen and rule England himself. After hours of breast-beating and cabinet meetings, the government decided to make Edward the Governor of the Bahamas, and to watch very carefully to make sure they didn't do anything too stupid.

Britain stood alone after France fell and was held together by Churchill's determined will and radio broadcasts, and that peculiar British spirit.

Everybody dug in and refused to believe they could be beaten, made fun of the Germans, grew vegetables and kept chickens. The British army got stuck in Dunkirk, and in a very British way, was saved by everyone in England who had a seaworthy boat sailng over to Dunkirk to get them back.

I honestly believe the people that enjoyed the war most were boys like my ex-husband and my brother, who were about ten when it started and were in a relatively safe area. They knew exactly what was happening everywhere, with maps and flags showing where army divisions were and what various ships were doing, while collecting all sorts of military paraphernalia. They were as organised as any general, probably more so than some. I always felt it was quite dangerous to go into my brother's bedroom in case he was harbouring a bomb of some kind. There were planes hanging from bits of string, bits of shrapnel, dead hand grenades and God knows what else or where he got it all from. In Palestine, my ex was apparently doing the same, only he actually had an army to play with. Part of the Australian troops on their way to Serai had a sort of recreation camp nearby. As he could speak some English, he used to go to the camp and chat with the soldiers.

During the first part of the Blitz, we were living in the country so I missed it. But we were in London for the second half, and I remember when the first doodlebug came over. These flying bombs, the V-1 and then the V-2 were creepy. We were used to hearing the planes come over and we'd start counting until we heard the bombs fall. Not so with the doodlebugs. There was just silence and then they landed and were much louder than the other bombs. When the first one landed no one knew what it was, so the authorities announced that it was a gasworks exploding, so from then on as they rained down people would say, "There goes another gasworks."

In 1942 the Japanese bombed Pearl Harbour, which I think was extremely stupid of them. To that point the Americans had stayed out of the war, but from then on in they came in, guns blazing.

We were still living in the country, when an American air force base was organised nearby. Even as a very small child I seemed to realise how very young those airmen were. One of them, the youngest of the group, used to play kids' games with me. His name was Apple. He was killed on his first bombing raid. I remember how upset we all were; I cried for days.

Meanwhile, the Australian were having a very hard time of it with the Japanese in the Philippines and Malaysia. Hong Kong and Singapore fell early in the piece. Nobody thought anyone could get at Singapore but the Japanese arrived. On bicycles. Something in their character made them very brutal fighters. And, as far as I'm concerned, quite mad. Their pilots were sent off on kamikaze raids, with instructions along the line of, "Off you go and don't come back". I mean, really?

Obviously, I've left out an enormous amount of battles all over the place, and, hopefully, what I have I have written about is correct. By 1943 the Allies were getting ready to invade Europe, but the Germans were aware that there was some sort of plan afoot. The Americans and the British came up with a very clever idea. They took a dead body, dressed it up as a marine commander and added a mysterious prop, so it appeared the corpse was carrying a briefcase full of top-secret information. They released him from a submarine and let him float away. He ended up on a Spanish beach. It worked brilliantly. The misinformation contained in the briefcase included elaborate plans for the Allies to land in Greece and Sardinia. Hitler believed every word. They made a great film about it called "The Man That Never Was".

The organising of D-Day was unbelievably complicated. I remember watching streams of tanks, armoured vehicles and God knows what, all heavily camouflaged, rumbling down country lanes in what looked like a never-ending procession.

D-Day 6th June 1944 was when the Allies started to take back Europe. It was an incredible mix of people, Americans, British, Canadians and the Free French in the air and on the sea. It's far to complicated for me to go into, but my ex's cousin (Roman Kawalek), who was a doctor, ended up on Omaha Beach in charge of his unit and he became a major (because everyone else above him was killed). Roman always liked being a soldier. When he died, they buried him at Arlington with full military honours, his son said, "If he'd know they were going to make all this fuss, he'd have died years ago".

CHAPTER 58

The Second Front

As the Americans, British, and Canadians set about organising D-Day, the Russians were getting heartily sick of the Germans battering them and Stalin told Churchill they had to open a second front. Montgomery was in charge of the British involvement on D-Day, but Eisenhower was in complete charge of the whole thing. A friend of mine's father, Field Marshal Alexander, was chief of Southern Command and had previously led the charge from El Alemain. On the opposing side was Field Marshal Erwin Rommel, nicknamed "The Desert Fox". (He was not a Nazi and took part in a plot to assassinate Hitler, and was subsequently forced to suicide by the Gestapo.) General Alexander was then made Commander in the Chief Mediterranean Theatre of War. General George S. Patton who commanded the Seventh United States Army in the Mediterranean tended to march to the beat of his own drum. Jointly under both, Sicily was invaded. This worked out alright in the end, but caused a lot of confusion at the time.

Patton's men adored him. They called him "Old Blood and Guts". To add to the melee, he apparently took Marlene Dietrich along for the ride (but not before teaching her how to shoot a gun and telling her that if the Germans caught her, she was to shoot herself).

Troops under Alexander swept across Italy and captured Rome, capturing towns without waiting for orders. People liked Alexander; he tended not to be carting film stars around with him, and was very organised in what he did, even if he didn't always inform other people beforehand.

The Italian campaign was very bloody, and basically a mess. Somehow anything with Italian involvement tends to be a mess, but they were finally defeated, or rather the Italians defeated themselves. They decided all this bloodshed and fighting was not for them. They hanged Mussolini, who had apparently made the trains run on time, but that was not all that was expected of a leader. Having got rid of Mussolini, the Italians changed sides. Most of them ended up in prisoner of war camps. Quite a lot came to England and Australia, where they seemed to be quite happy working on farms. When the war was finally over, many of them didn't want to go home.

Apropos nothing in particular, except in an odd sort of way, I was in New York, and a friend of mine, Stewart Stern went to see a play. (Stewart was really "Hollywood Royalty", the nephew of Adolf Zukor - who founded Paramount Pictures - as well as being a bloody good writer, having written "Rebel Without a Cause", among other things). In the interval we bumped into Michael Strong, an actor who was up for a part in Stewart's latest movie, but he hadn't got it and was aware of the fact. Deep gloom had set in. Try as we might, Stewart and I couldn't lift it. We suggested he come to supper with us. My ex joined us, took one look at Michael and said. "I know you. You were General something or other in "Patton". You were terrific". The gloom vanished as if it had never been. Michael felt he was a star with fans, and everything was alright again with the world. To this day, my ex has no idea how or why he suddenly became Michael's new best friend. Stewart and I looked at each other and shrugged, we could have done that hours ago if only we'd thought of it.

Now, let's get back to World War history, shall we? Well, simply put, D-Day and the Second Front were really "the end of the beginning", as Churchill said. It began to occur to the Germans they might not win. It was a moot point whether destroying whole cities was really the answer to finishing the war. The Germans had flattened Coventry, Liverpool and parts of London, so the British flattened Dresden; which looking back was not a great idea. VE-Day (Victory in Europe) was 8th May 1945, when the Germans formally surrendered.

The Australian Army was caught up in some very bloody fighting with the Japanese. They were like terriers refusing to let go. The prisoner of war camp at Changi was dreadful. The Japanese surrendered early August 1945 after the second atomic bomb was dropped on Nagasaki. However, some Japanese soldiers in the jungles on the Pacific Islands would not believe the war was over and just went on fighting, refusing to surrender.

Americans finally won on all fronts.

As for the rest of history... Well, you have probably lived through much of that for yourselves - or seen it on television - and don't need me to tell you about it.

www.ingramcontent.com/pod-product-compliance
Lightning Source LLC
LaVergne TN
LVHW021712060526
838200LV00050B/2624